Georgia

Georgia

Nancy Robinson Masters

Children's Press®
A Division of Grolier Publishing
New York   London   Hong Kong   Sydney
Danbury, Connecticut

Frontispiece: Amicalola Falls in the Chattahoochee National Forest

Front cover: The Atlanta skyline at night

Back cover: Mount Yonah

Consultant: Jennie Williams, Atlanta History Center

Please note: All statistics are as up-to-date as possible at the time of publication.

Visit Children's Press on the Internet at http://publishing.grolier.com

Book production by Editorial Directions, Inc.

Library of Congress Cataloging-in-Publication Data

Robinson Masters, Nancy
    Georgia / Nancy Robinson Masters.
      p. cm. — (America the beautiful. Second series)
    Includes bibliographical references and index.
    Summary : An introduction to the geography, history, natural resources, economy, culture, people, and interesting sites of the state of Georgia.
    ISBN 0-516-20685-0
    1. Georgia—Juvenile literature. [1. Georgia.] I. Title. II. Series.
F286.3.R63 1999
978.8—dc21
                              98-14036
                                 CIP
                                 AC

Acknowledgments

The author expresses her appreciation for research assistance provided by the Georgia Humanities Council and the staff of the Office of the Governor of Georgia.

Canola field

Cotton

Atlanta Underground

Contents

Sequoya

Kudzu

Cumberland Island horses

Shrimp processing

Peaches and peanuts

Chapter One

A New Settlement

Mary Musgrove hurriedly wrapped the deerskin boots over her feet. The *Anne* was arriving from England. She knew she had to move quickly to get to Yamacraw Bluff in time to meet the ship.

Half Creek Indian and half English, Mary was also known by her Indian name, *Coosaponakesee*. She was a native of Coweta, the Creek capital on the Chattahoochee River. Coosaponakesee had been sent to South Carolina when she was seven years old to be educated in English schools. She was given the name *Mary* when she was baptized into the Church of England. She married John Musgrove, an English settler, when she was sixteen. The couple established a trading post between Alabama and South Carolina, and Mary's knowledge of both native and English ways made them very successful.

Mary's business and political skills were respected throughout the territory. Her skills as a translator, however, would be most needed this twelfth day of February, 1733. Word had come from traders in Charles Towne that Englishmen were arriving on the *Anne* to establish a new settlement below Yamacraw Bluff on the Savannah River. The leader of the settlers was a man named James Edward Oglethorpe.

Mary knew that Yamacraw chief Tomochichi would be watching from the bluff overlooking the Savannah River. The Yamacraw tribe had separated from the Creek, but she and old Chief

James Edward Oglethorpe was a British general who settled the colony of Georgia.

Opposite: Along the Savannah River where James Oglethorpe sailed

King George II of England, for whom Georgia was named

Tomochichi had remained friends. If Oglethorpe wanted to establish an English settlement, he would need to secure a peaceful agreement with the chief—and he would need Mary as his translator.

Mary's excitement grew with each step. A new group of English colonists moving into the territory would mean more customers for the Musgrove trading post. It would also help ensure resistance to the Spanish who wanted to control the area that once had been traveled only by the Creek, Cherokee, Choctaw, Chickasaw, Seminole, Timucuan, Gaule, Yamacraw, Yamsee, and the long-departed Ancient People.

Mary knew that she would need her best skills to ensure that Oglethorpe and the 114 people arriving with him were welcomed. Moving steadily forward along the trail, she practiced saying aloud the name the English had chosen for the new settlement in honor of their king: "Georgia."

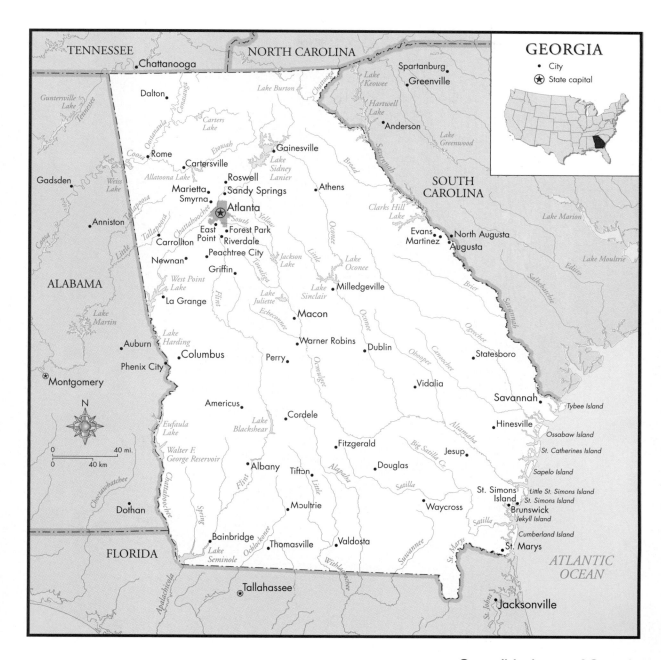

Geopolitical map of Georgia

CHAPTER TWO

People and Pathways of the Past

Before James Edward Oglethorpe arrived, some 10,000 Cherokee and Creek natives were believed to be living in what was to become Georgia. The Creeks dominated the coastal and plains regions; the Cherokee occupied the lower Appalachian Mountain region to the north. These native people were actually latecomers to the area, however. Three earlier civilizations had already left footprints on the trail that Mary Musgrove walked along to meet the Englishmen arriving on the *Anne.*

The Archaic Period

The earliest pottery in North America has been found at Stallings Island in the Savannah River. These Paleo-Indian artifacts belonged to nomadic hunters living during what is known as the Archaic Period (9000–1000 B.C.). They were descendants of Asian groups who migrated across the Bering Strait to North America 50,000 years ago.

The Creek Indians were one of the five Native American nations in southeastern Georgia when the Europeans arrived.

These nomads were also Georgia's first farmers. Evidence of crop cultivation has been found in this same area.

The Woodland Period

Permanent villages with farms and regular trade networks were spread across Georgia during the Woodland Period (1000 B.C.–

Opposite: Settlers in early Georgia

A.D 900). This culture was part of a larger network of civilizations reaching from the Gulf of Mexico to the Great Lakes.

During this period, the first aboriginal earthworks were built. Some of these huge mounds of dirt were built as grave sites. Others, like the 56-foot (17-m)-high Kolomoki Mound near Blakely, were used as ceremonial platforms.

The Mississippian Period

Growing corn, beans, and squash was an important part of the lives of the Mississippians who displaced the Woodland People. Farming these crops—known as the Three Sisters— helped sustain the Mississippians from A.D. 900–1200. These people also utilized plant materials and hunted the abundant population of deer and other wildlife.

The end of the Mississippian Period was followed by the emergence of the Lamar culture, a blending of the cultures of various native peoples, which dominated the region until the seventeenth century.

Spanish Hoofbeats

In 1540, Spanish explorer Hernando de Soto led 600 horses and 900 soldiers through Georgia in search of gold. Unknown to de Soto, as he traveled across the northern region, his horses' hooves tromped directly over rich deposits of the very ore he sought.

Before encountering the Cherokee in their northern strongholds, de Soto had crossed paths with the Timucuan in the south of the region, the Guale along the

Spanish explorer Hernando de Soto searched unsuccessfully for gold in Georgia.

Mound Bound

Three of the most interesting archaeological sites east of the Mississippi River are found in Georgia. Each year, these sites attract thousands of "mound hounds" who come to study the mounds of dirt and the circles of piled shells. The mounds were used for ceremonies and burials; some may have served as navigational guides.

The 683 acres (276 ha) of Ocmulgee National Monument near Macon were occupied by humans from 10,000 B.C. to the early eighteenth century. Seven mounds built by the Mississippians are on the site. Among the rare artifacts that have been found at Ocmulgee is a copper-covered puma jawbone.

The seven mounds in Kolomoki Mounds State Park near Blakely were built during the twelfth and thirteenth centuries by the Swift Creek and Weeden Indians. The mounds include Georgia's oldest temple mound, two burial mounds, and four ceremonial mounds.

Etowah Indian Mounds (above) near Cartersville contains the largest mound in the southern Appalachian Mountains. It stands 63 feet (19.2 m) tall and covers 3 acres (1.2 ha). This site is among the most important archaeological finds in North America. ■

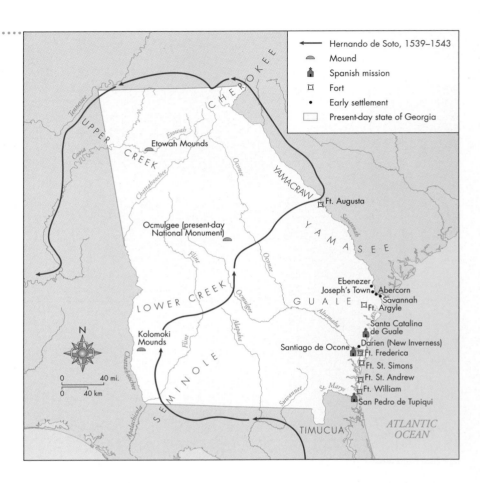

Exploration of Georgia

coast, and the Creek in the central plain. The sound of de Soto's horses was the death knell for thousands of these native people. The Indians had no natural immunity to the diseases brought by the Europeans. Measles and flu killed more than half of the population.

The gold that de Soto sought but never found remained undiscovered for three more centuries.

When the Dust Settled

French Huguenots who were fleeing religious persecution arrived on Georgia's barrier islands twenty-two years after de Soto had left. In an effort to stop the French, who were intent upon claiming lands

Descendants of the Spanish soldiers' horses still roam free on Cumberland Island.

east of the Mississippi, the Spanish built forts known as *presidios*. These forts also provided protection from the Indians.

When the Spanish soldiers moved farther inland in an attempt to expand their claims, Spanish missionaries occupied the forts. By 1686, the missionaries had abandoned the islands, leaving behind fig, orange, peach, and olive orchards. They also left horses, whose descendants still roam Cumberland Island.

Meet Me in Savannah

"More meetings have taken place on Savannah's behalf than for any other city in the New World," writes Roulhac B. Toledano in *The National Trust Guide to Savannah*.

The meetings about Savannah began in London, England, in about 1730. Twenty-one men known as the Georgia Trustees volunteered to plan a new British colony in America. These men—one of whom was James Edward Oglethorpe—came from a wide range of backgrounds, but they shared a common goal. They wanted to develop a colony of small farmers, merchants, and soldiers who

Lord John Percival, one of the Georgia Trustees

James Edward Oglethorpe

James Edward Oglethorpe (1696–1785), the tenth child of Eleanor and Theophiles Oglethorpe, was born on December 22 in London, England. He served in the British army and became a military hero. Following in his father's and brother's footsteps, he was elected to Parliament in 1722.

In 1729, Oglethorpe chaired the committee that legislated British prison reforms. In 1732, he and twenty other men obtained a charter from King George II to establish the colony of Georgia, named in honor of the king. In 1733, at the age of thirty-six, he accompanied the first group of colonists and established the first English settlement at Savannah. In 1743, he returned to England and married Elizabeth Wright.

In 1745, the British army promoted Oglethorpe to major general and, in 1765, to general. He continued to raise funds for and encourage settlement of Georgia until his death. ■

would support themselves without slave labor. The colony would provide a place where debtors released from London prisons could build a new life. Those being persecuted for their religious beliefs in Europe—such as the Quakers and Mennonites—would be able to practice their faith in freedom in the new colony.

Boundary Treaties

Georgia's present-day borders were established through many treaties signed over the course of more than one hundred years.

1763 Spain cedes Florida to England and establishes Georgia's boundary at St. Marys River. France gives all the land east of the Mississippi River to the colony. Georgia's boundaries with the Creek Nation are established.

1783 Northern boundary is extended along the 35th parallel, from Nickerjack Creek 140 miles (225 km) east to the Chattooga River.

1787 Border with South Carolina is established.

1802 Georgia cedes to the United States all the land west of the Chattahoochee River and Nickajack Creek and north of the 31st parallel.

1866 Border with Florida is established.

1883 Boundary with Alabama is established. ■

The charter granted by King George II to "the Trustees for Establishing the Colony of Georgia in America" was good for twenty-one years. It defined the area of the new colony as the land between the Savannah and Altamaha Rivers, "inland to their headwaters and then westward to the south seas [the Pacific Ocean]."

Funding the Colony

Funds to establish the colony of Georgia came through private donations and from the British Parliament. The new colony would serve as an important buffer between Spanish-held Florida to the south and the British colony of South Carolina to the north.

The trustees were certain that the colony would succeed both as a social experiment and as a defense against the Spanish and the French. The success, they believed, would generate more private donations to sustain the colony until it could sustain itself.

The British Parliament helped to fund the Georgia colony.

Oglethorpe's Grand Plan

Because of Mary Musgrove's translation skills, James Oglethorpe and Chief Tomochichi soon became close friends. Agreements were reached that allowed Oglethorpe to lay out the town of Savannah on 15,000 acres (6,070 ha) of land that the Spanish had named *sabana,* "flat country."

Oglethorpe's plan divided the land into *wards,* each with a center *square.* The squares served as stockyards and as places of

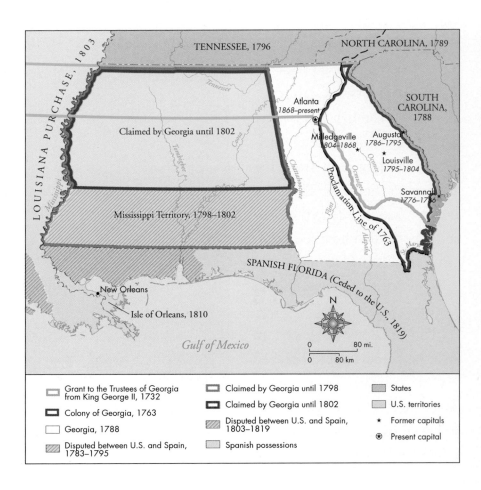

Historical map of Georgia

James Oglethorpe and Chief Tomochichi discussing a fur trade

safety during attacks. Each square would be flanked by *trust lots*—two on its east side and two on its west side. These trust lots were reserved for public buildings, churches, schools, and community and civic institutions.

Residences were organized in *tithing blocks.* Each tithing block consisted of ten lots laid out to the north and south sides of each square. Each tithing lot had a 5-acre (2-ha) garden lot and a farm of almost 45 acres (18 ha).

The distribution of the first 5-acre (2-ha) parcels took place on July 7, 1733. Although the trustees had prohibited women from receiving land grants, Mary Musgrove eventually received a grant of 500 acres (202.5 ha) for her services as translator.

Battle of Bloody Marsh

On July 7, 1742, James Oglethorpe led his colonists to a stunning victory against Spanish soldiers. The battle became known as the Battle of Bloody Marsh.

The colonists surprised the Spanish in a marshland along a narrow trail a few miles from Fort Frederica on St. Simons Island. The Spanish retreated to Florida, and they were never again a threat to the English in Georgia. The Battle of Bloody Marsh has been called one of the most decisive battles in American history. ■

Road to Revolution

By 1774, rumblings from northern colonies that favored separation from British rule reached Georgia. Many of the people living in Georgia, however, were loyal to the British Crown and did not support the idea of separation. On September 24, 1774, a colonist living in a Quaker settlement wrote in the *Georgia Gazette* (the first newspaper begun in Georgia in 1763): "We take exception to the cause of those who wish to rebel against the King." A year later, however, this pro-British sentiment was not as widespread. In 1775, Georgia joined the Union of Colonies.

When the Declaration of Independence was signed in Philadelphia on July 4, 1776, three Georgians put their signatures on the document: Button Gwinnett, a merchant; Lyman Hall, a doctor later elected governor of Georgia; and George Walton (right), an attorney. At

age thirty-five, Walton was one of the youngest men to sign the Declaration of Independence. ■

In addition to Savannah, Oglethorpe founded the cities of Augusta and Darien. He established Fort Frederica and a line of forts along the 100-mile (161-km) coast between Savannah and St. Augustine, Spain's northernmost outpost in what is now Florida.

Returning Home

Oglethorpe returned to England three times to raise money for the new colony. On his first trip, he raised a large sum by convincing Parliament that money was needed to fortify Georgia's border against the threat of the French who had settled along the Gulf of Mexico. Oglethorpe's concerns about the French were based on personal knowledge. His two sisters, Fanny and Eleanor, had married wealthy Frenchmen and were involved in bringing French settlers to Louisiana.

In 1734, Chief Tomochichi and his nephew Toonahowi traveled with Oglethorpe on another voyage back to England. The two men were introduced to the king and treated as American royalty.

In 1743, Oglethorpe made his final trip to England. He never set foot in Georgia again, although he continued to seek financial support for the struggling colony. In 1752, the trustees reluctantly returned the charter to King George II, and in 1754, Georgia became a royal province.

Georgia's State Capitals

Atlanta, the present-day capital, is the fifth city to be designated the capital of Georgia. Several other cities have also served as temporary seats of government; these are indicated by an *.

1777–1778	Savannah
1779–1780	Augusta*
1780–1781	Heard's Fort*, miscellaneous sites in Wilkes County*
1781–1782	Augusta
1782	Ebenezer*, Savannah
1783	Augusta
1784	Savannah, Augusta
1785	Savannah
1786–1796	Augusta
1796–1806	Louisville
1807–1864	Milledgeville
1864–1865	Macon*
1865–1868	Milledgeville
1868–present	Atlanta ■

Revolutionary Heroine

There are many stories and myths about Georgia's fierce freedom fighter, Nancy Morgan Hart. According to legend, she was 6 feet (1.8 m) tall, with red hair and a fiery temper. She was a skilled doctor and an excellent shot. The neighboring Indians called her War Woman, out of respect. Some say she was first cousin to Daniel Boone.

Although she also took care of a family, home, and farm, Hart often worked as a spy during the Revolutionary War. She gained entry into British soldier camps—one time, by pretending to be crazy; another, by pretending to be a poor woman selling eggs—and reported the valuable information she gathered about the enemy's locations and plans to the patriots.

Legend has it that, one day, five British soldiers arrived at the Hart's log cabin. Nancy was alone; her husband, Benjamin, and the children were working in the fields. Nancy good-naturedly prepared food for the soldiers, but while they were eating, she slipped their rifles through the holes in the cabin's mud-chinked walls. When the soldiers realized what she was doing, they tried to stop her. She grabbed a rifle and shot two soldiers. When Ben and the other men who had been working in the fields returned to the cabin, they hung the rest of the soldiers.

In 1912, skeletons were unearthed during the grading of the railroad near the site of the Hart cabin. The bones were proven to be the remains of the soldiers shot by Nancy Hart.

Nancy Hart Historical Park in Elbert County contains a replica of the Hart cabin, with stones from the original fireplace and chimney, erected on the original home site. The park regularly hosts Pioneer Day, an educational and recreational family event, which includes the Nancy Hart Drama, a Look-a-Like Contest, and demonstrations of pioneer life skills.

Hart County is the only county in Georgia named for a woman. ■

Rough Times

The Revolutionary War (1775–1783), which followed the colonists' declaration of independence, created terrible hardships for the people of Georgia. There were only about 2,000 men available to fight. Between battles, they had to keep their farms and businesses going. By the end of 1779, every important town in Georgia had fallen under control of the British.

When American patriot forces ran the last of the British troops out of Savannah in 1782, almost half of the state's private property had been destroyed. The state treasury was empty.

The people of Georgia did not look back on their losses. In September 1787, two men from Georgia were sent as delegates to the Constitutional Convention in Philadelphia: Abraham Baldwin and William Few. They signed the Constitution of the United States of America, the document that established the nation. The people of Georgia ratified (voted to accept and abide by) the Constitution, and on January 2, 1788, Georgia became the fourth of the thirteen original colonies to become a state.

CHAPTER THREE

Troubled Times

The first cotton gin

There will be less need for slaves and more time for socials," a Georgia teenager wrote to her cousin in 1793. The Georgia girl had just seen Eli Whitney's new invention, the cotton engine. The "gin" could separate the seeds from the cotton fibers faster and better than the slaves on the plantations could do the work by hand.

Slavery did not begin in Georgia—or even in the United States. The practice of treating humans as if they were possessions has been part of many world civilizations throughout history. When Georgia was founded, slavery was banned in the colony. James Oglethorpe and the other trustees believed slavery was contrary to the purpose of the colony's charter: "to relieve the distressed." Oglethorpe also wanted settlers who could serve as soldiers, and he feared armed slaves might rebel.

Despite the plan to keep Georgia free of slavery, economic pressures from neighboring slaveholding colonies led to the repeal of the prohibition against slavery in 1749. By 1791, one-third of Georgia's population were slaves. Communities of "free men of color" also existed in Georgia. These communities were made up of former slaves who had either bought their freedom or been manumitted (released).

Opposite: Cotton has been an important part of Georgia's past and present.

Spinning Cotton

The trustees had believed that Georgia's wild mulberry trees would produce the new colony's most important product: silkworms. By 1750, however, there were no silkworm farms or silk production in Georgia. Planters had turned to cotton. In 1791, Georgia produced a thousand bales of cotton—mostly through the use of slave labor.

In 1793, Eli Whitney was traveling by stagecoach when he met the widow of Revolutionary War hero General Nathaniel Greene. She invited Whitney to visit Mulberry Grove, the Greene's cotton plantation in Savannah. There, Whitney observed the difficulty the slaves had separating the cotton seed from the fibers. Whitney began designing a machine that could do in one hour what it took several slave workers to accomplish in ten.

With the invention of the cotton gin in 1793, Georgia's cotton production skyrocketed. In 1801, the state produced 20,000 bales; in 1826, it sold 150,000 bales. By 1860, Georgia's annual cotton production peaked at more than 700,000 bales of "white gold."

Wheels of Change

The cotton gin was not the only invention that helped move America toward industrialization. In 1819, the steamship *Savannah* became the first steam-powered ship to cross the Atlantic Ocean, sailing from Savannah to Liverpool, England. Everything from sewing machines to grain reapers were revolutionizing the way people lived and worked.

In 1819, the *Savannah* became the first steamship to cross the Atlantic Ocean.

Not everyone embraced all the new mechanical inventions. Plantation owners in Georgia and other Southern states felt that human slaves were still the best solution for their labor needs.

One slave trader's advertisements claimed "a mule and a man" were all that was needed to make a Georgia farmer successful.

Prior to 1860, most "plantations" in Georgia were actually farms of fewer than 100 acres (40.5 ha). These 31,000 farms operated almost entirely without slave labor, compared to the few hundred farms of more than 1,000 acres (405 ha) that did use slaves.

Although slavery existed in the Northern states, some Northerners began speaking out against slavery. A few opposed it on moral grounds. Many simply feared that slave labor would cost them their livelihoods by taking work away from them. At the same time, people in the South were horrified by stories of Northern cities, where immigrants were forced to work eighteen hours a day in windowless factories to repay the cost of their ship passages to America.

Fire-Eater

"Secede!" Senator Robert Augustus Toombs (1810–1885) wanted Georgia out of the Union. On January 19, 1861, his "fire-eating" verbal campaign paid off. By a vote of 108 to 89, Georgia left the Union. Delegates from Georgia voted to join the Confederate States of America (CSA). Jefferson Davis (1808–1889), a popular U.S. senator from Mississippi, was elected president of the CSA.

Northerners called for war against the Southern Confederacy. On April 12, 1861—when U.S. troops refused to withdraw from Fort Sumter, South Carolina—the South replied. From the shores of Charleston, a 6,000-man Confederate army bombarded the fort with cannons. The American Civil War (1861–1865), also called the War between the States, was underway.

Senator Robert Toombs, who encouraged Georgia to secede from the Union in 1861

Confederates in Company K

More than 120,000 men and boys from Georgia served in the Confederate Army. Camp Bailey, located between Fairburn and Palmetto, was typical of the Confederate camps established to train farm boys to fight as soldiers. In 1861, volunteers were recruited from Campbell and Carroll Counties to train at Camp Bailey and serve as members of Company K.

Most of the Georgia boys who volunteered were between seventeen and twenty-one years old; some were even younger. They believed that the war would only last a few months.

Life in Company K was not easy. Every meal consisted of salt pork, dried beans, and hardtack. The hardtack, tough biscuits made of flour and water, was nicknamed iron crackers.

A soldier in Company K had no way to escape the heat, insects, odors, or unclean conditions of the camp. To take a bath or wash the only suit of clothing he had was a rare opportunity. Most men preferred to sleep outside on the ground rather than inside a tent with ten other bad-smelling soldiers.

The men rose at daylight. In addition to fighting, they had to care for the mules, chop wood for cooking, and keep their shoes repaired. A barefoot soldier had a hard time keeping up when it was time to break camp and move on.

Company K fought in the battles at Calhoun, New Hope Church, Kennesaw, and Jonesboro. They fought all the way to Nashville, Tennessee, where they were captured and taken to Camp Chase, a Union prison camp in Ohio. Few of the men of Company K ever returned to Georgia. Many starved to death or died from exposure to the extreme cold of the North.

A Soldier's Recipe for Hoe Cakes

"Mix one pint of cornmeal with cold water and one teaspoon of salt. Make a stiff dough. Dust iron hoe blade with meal and lay thin batter on blade. Hold blade over fire until cornmeal begins to pop. Do not use butter on hoe as it will scorch too quickly.

"Always cook more than you can eat to carry with you. You may be in enemy territory or rain where cooking fires cannot be built." ■

National Prisoner of War Museum

Camp Sumter in Andersonville, Georgia, was the largest of the Confederate prison camps. During its fourteen months of operation, 45,000 Union soldiers were housed there, and 13,000 died.

In 1998, the National Park Service opened the National Prisoner of War Museum at the Andersonville site. The museum honors all Americans who have lost their freedom during times of war. ■

Battlefield Medicine

Many Civil War casualties resulted from unsanitary conditions in battlefield hospitals. Three out of every four wounded soldiers were shot in arms or legs. Amputation was the only medical treatment known to stop infection in a serious wound from spreading. Surgeons, however, might spend an entire day removing arms and legs without ever cleaning their knives. Many soldiers—some with even relatively minor wounds—died or became permanently disabled because of infections or other complications caused by the surgery itself.

Dr. Crawford W. Long

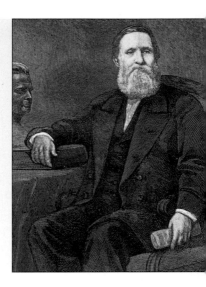

Crawford W. Long (1815–1878) was born in Danielsville, Georgia. He graduated from the University of Georgia, received his medical degree from the University of Pennsylvania in 1839, and studied surgery in New York City.

After finishing his studies, Long returned to Georgia and set up his practice in Jefferson. He experimented with sulfuric ether as an anesthetic (pain suppressor) for patients having surgery. On March 30, 1842, he administered the substance to a patient for the first time, before surgically removing a tumor from a boy's neck.

Long did not publish the results of his operation until 1849. Several other doctors and dentists claimed to have been the first to use an anesthetic. Long, however, is recognized as the first to use one during surgery. ■

At the time of the Civil War, ether and chloroform were commonly used anesthetics (substances that reduce physical sensation). Lack of supplies on the battlefield, however, forced most soldiers to undergo amputations without any medication. Civil War veterans who were missing arms or legs were often referred to as soldiers who had "suffered the agony of being saved by the saw."

The Battle of Chickamauga Creek

Although the Union had seized all of the state's coastal islands in 1862, Georgia had been spared much of the heavy fighting during the first three years of the Civil War. The Battle of Chickamauga Creek in northwestern Georgia was an exception. General Braxton Bragg's Confederates forced Union general William Rosecrans to retreat—but only after 18,000 Confederate and 16,000 Union soldiers were killed or wounded in the bloodiest two days of the entire Civil War.

Thomas Jonathan "Stonewall" Jackson

Thomas Jonathan Jackson (1824–1863), who earned the nickname Stonewall during the Battle of Bull Run, grew up as a poor orphan. He suffered from what is now known as dyslexia and disciplined himself to memorize everything he heard. He graduated seventeenth in a class of fifty-nine from the U.S. Military Academy at West Point.

Jackson was one of many Civil War soldiers who died as a result of complications following a limb amputation. He was riding with his officers at dusk following the Confederate victory at Chancellorsville when one of his own men mistook him for the enemy and shot him. Following the amputation of his arm, Jackson caught pneumonia and died. ■

The March to the Sea

Georgia suffered its worst devastation of the war in November 1864. Union general William Tecumseh Sherman (1820–1891) and his troops had captured Atlanta two months earlier. On November 15, the general launched a 50-mile (80 km)-wide march of total destruction from Atlanta to Savannah. Before leaving Atlanta for their famous march to the sea, Sherman ordered his soldiers to set fire to the city. All but 400 of Atlanta's 4,000 buildings were reduced to ashes.

On April 9, 1865, Confederate general Robert E. Lee (1807–1870) surrendered the South to Union general Ulysses S. Grant (1822–1885). By then, more than 620,000 Americans from

both sides had been killed. The South, however, had suffered the greatest destruction to its homes, farms, and businesses. The South had also suffered a tremendous loss of its male population. The 1870 census showed there were 36,000 more women than men living in Georgia.

General Sherman's fiery march through Atlanta in 1864

Letters from Home

The Civil War caused the largest outpouring of correspondence in American history. Estimates are that as many as 300,000 letters a day passed through postal offices and traveled by military couriers. Most letters were written in pencil. If paper was unavailable, letters were written on pieces of wallpaper, dried tobacco leaves, and corn shucks.

Confederate stamps featured portraits of President Jefferson Davis and General Thomas J. "Stonewall" Jackson. These historically important stamps are especially prized by collectors today. ■

John Henry Holliday

John Henry "Doc" Holliday (1852–1887) was one of the many people who left Georgia shortly after the end of the Civil War. Some claim that the legendary dentist-turned-gunfighter left Georgia after killing a man during an argument. Others say he escaped after being accused of being involved in a plot to blow up the federally occupied Lowndes County Courthouse.

Holliday's friendship with frontier lawman Wyatt Earp took him to Arizona and the famous gunfight with the Clanton gang at the O.K. Corral in Tombstone. Holliday traveled to Colorado seeking treatment for tuberculosis and died in Glenwood Springs. ■

The Fifteenth Amendment

The years immediately following the Civil War, known as the Reconstruction period, were turbulent in Georgia. The state was allowed to reenter the Union in 1868, but it was expelled in 1869 because it refused to ratify the Fifteenth Amendment of the Constitution. The amendment made it illegal to deny the right to vote on the basis of race.

Roving "carpetbaggers" from the North, seeking to profit from the misfortunes of both blacks and whites, added to the racial tensions. Many people left Georgia searching for new lives in the expanding American West.

On February 2, 1870, Georgia finally ratified the amendment. On July 15, Georgia was permanently readmitted to the United States, with all the rights of statehood restored. The New South had been born.

Henry Woodfin Grady

Henry Woodfin Grady (1850–1889) was born in Athens, Georgia, and graduated from the University of Georgia in 1868. He worked as the Georgia correspondent for a New York newspaper before borrowing money in 1880 to buy an interest in the *Atlanta Constitution*.

Grady served as the newspaper's chief editor and campaigned for cooperation between the North and the South. He is credited for coining the term *New South* to emphasize Georgia's move away from its former plantation economy. ■

Rising Again

In the years between 1870 and 1900, Georgia experienced some of its greatest triumphs and its greatest tragedies. Moving from the devastation of the Civil War to the realities of life in the New South brought changes, good and bad.

The South had been split into five military districts, and Atlanta was the headquarters of the third military district. Federal troops continued to occupy the city for the better part of ten years.

A decline in the world's demand for cotton forced many landowners to become sharecroppers. They had to borrow money to grow a crop, but then received only a portion of the proceeds from the harvest, which made it impossible for them to ever repay the loan.

"The farmers may farm as wisely as they please, but as long as we manufacture nothing and rely on the shops, mills and factories of other sections for everything we use, our section must remain dependent and poor," wrote editor Henry Woodfin Grady in the *Atlanta Constitution*.

Grady promoted crop diversification for Georgia farmers, and he pushed Georgia toward industrialization. His efforts brought to Atlanta expanding rail networks, manufacturing business, and investors from the North. At the same time, segregation took a firm hold with the so-called Jim Crow laws, which were designed to force separate and unequal treatment for blacks.

Voting restrictions, violence, and openly expressed hostility toward blacks dominated the judicial systems at all levels. Politically sanctioned racism reigned in Georgia.

In 1895, the International Cotton States Exposition opened in Atlanta. Just thirty years after Sherman left Atlanta in ashes, the city invited the world to come and see how it had risen again. More than one million visitors strolled the land where Sherman had marched. Instead of ashes, the visitors saw an Atlanta that was thriving—and moving Georgia into the twentieth century.

Set in Stone

Today, three of the South's greatest Civil War heroes are honored at Stone Mountain Park north of Atlanta. The likenesses of Jefferson Davis, Robert E. Lee, and "Stonewall" Jackson—all mounted on horseback—are engraved in the world's largest piece of sculpture cut into the world's greatest mass of granite.

In 1915, the United Daughters of the Confederacy leased the land occupied by Stone Mountain to create a carving on the side of the mountain. When the lease expired in 1927, only the faces of Lee and Davis had been cut. The carving remained unfinished until 1958 when the Georgia legislature created the Stone Mountain Memorial Association to develop it as a tourist attraction.

Chief carver Roy Faulkner became involved with the project in 1964, forty-nine years after it began. Faulkner spent 3,140 days—more than eight years of his life—on the mountain. Faulkner, who had never had an art lesson, experimented with a new carving tool, a thermo-jet torch that could remove several tons of granite a day. Each morning, he would make notes from the master model and then go up the mountain to work on the carving. On March 3, 1972, Faulkner finished the job.

More than 5 million people travel to the 3,200-acre (1,296-ha) recreation park every year to see Stone Mountain. Regardless of the Civil War's outcome, Davis, Lee, and Jackson will forever ride tall in the saddle.

A memorial to Davis, Lee, and Jackson is carved in the granite of Stone Mountain.

CHAPTER FOUR

The Twentieth Century and Onward

In the 1920s, the boll weevil had a devastating effect on Georgia's cotton fields.

n 1893, when fifteen-year-old Catherine Evans Whitener made her first cotton-tufted bedspread, she had no idea she was also making history. She sewed thick cotton yarns with a running stitch into unbleached muslin, clipped the ends of the yarn so they would fluff out, and then washed the spread in hot water to shrink the fabric and hold the yarns in place. Whitener began displaying her bedspreads for sale for $2.50 each on her front porch in Dalton, Georgia. Interest in her handwork grew.

As demand increased, more girls and women began making the tufted spreads to sell. By the end of World War I (1914–1918), an estimated 10,000 women were working for various companies at home and paid by the hour—in what is known as a cottage industry—making the tufted spreads by hand. These spreads sold for as much as $10 each. Many of the bedspreads were sold to travelers between Dalton and Cartersville on U.S. Highway 41, which became known as Bedspread Boulevard. The highway sales brought thousands of tourists and an improving economy to the New South.

Weevil War

One visitor to Georgia did not bring economic improvements. The insect *Anthonomus grandis*—better known as the boll weevil—invaded the state just before World War I. The snout-nosed weevils

Opposite: The 1895 Cotton States Exposition in Atlanta

marched through 5 million (2 million ha) acres of Georgia, destroying every cotton boll in their path. Cotton production fell from 2,122,000 bales in 1918 to 388,000 in 1923. Greene County, for example, produced 21,500 bales in 1919, but only 326 bales in 1922.

"The boll weevil did what Sherman and all the Union armies could not," one Mitchell County farmer said. Two out of ten Georgians (almost half a million people) left the state in the wake of the devastation.

Georgia was losing the battle with the boll weevil. In 1919, cotton sold for 35 cents a pound (half kilogram); in 1920, the price fell to 15 cents. When the New York Stock Market crash of 1929 sent the nation into the economic disaster known as the Great Depression, Georgia's economy was already on the verge of collapse.

In 1932, Franklin Delano Roosevelt (1882–1945) won the presidential election by proposing a plan to get America out of the Great Depression. His plan was known as the New Deal. The Wage and Hours Act, one of the New Deal laws passed in 1938, created a minimum wage of 25 cents an hour. For the women making tufted bedspreads in Dalton, who were being paid by the hour, the minimum-wage law made it too expensive to continue to produce the spreads by hand. They began using sewing machines adapted for tufting, which allowed them to produce more bedspreads in less time.

Eventually, mechanized tufting machines

Carpet Capital of the World

Each year, 1.1 billion square yards (0.9 billion sq m) of carpet are made in Georgia—that's enough carpet, 12 feet (3.7 m) wide, to wrap around Earth four times.

Approximately 55,000 people are employed in carpet manufacturing in Georgia. Another 28,000 are employed in related industries, such as machinery supplies. The carpet industry generates an annual payroll of $900 million for the workforce of Georgia. ■

were developed to produce bedspreads with finer tufts. These bedspread fabrics were called chenille. *Chenille* is the French word for "caterpillar." Hundreds of Georgia families survived the Great Depression working in chenille-bedspread factories.

After World War II, Georgia's textile industry expanded to include carpets and rugs woven on looms. By the mid-1950s, synthetic fibers, such as nylon, began to replace the cotton yarns. Today, the six largest carpet-manufacturing companies in the world have their headquarters in Georgia.

Collett Woolman, founder of Delta Airlines

Wings over Weevils

In 1924, the boll weevil finally met its match. Huff-Daland Dusters of Macon flew airplanes equipped with pesticides—known as crop dusters—over the cotton fields to destroy the invaders.

In 1928, Collett Woolman and his partners bought the Macon crop-dusting business, changed the name to Delta Airlines, and moved the operation to Atlanta Airfield. The airline began carrying passengers instead of pesticides.

William B. Hartsfield International Airport

William Berry Hartsfield was committed to the economic growth and prosperity of the city of Atlanta. In 1925, Mayor Walter A. Sims appointed Harts-field, who was then an alder-man, as the chairman of the city's new aviation committee. Hartsfield was instrumental in transforming Candler Field, an abandoned racetrack outside Hapeville, into a thriving trans-portation hub for the city.

Today, the William B. Harts-field International Airport's pas-senger terminal covers 130 acres (52.6 ha), including 24 international and 146 domestic gates, all connected by a 3.5 mile (5.6 km) underground sub-way. More than 66 million pas-sengers transit the airport each year, and there are an average of 2,100 takeoffs and landings each day.

There are approximately 33,000 employees. The airport generates $15 billion of revenue in Georgia each year and ranks as one of the top five airports in the nation. ■

Today, Delta Airlines is headquartered at the William B. Harts-field International Airport in Atlanta, one of the busiest airports in the world. The airport is named for William Berry Hartsfield (1890–1971), who served as mayor of Atlanta from 1937 to 1941 and from 1942 until 1961.

Women on the Move

In 1749, Mary Musgrove was forced to defend her rights as owner of Ossabaw, St. Catherines, and Sapelo Islands. She had purchased the coastal islands from her Creek cousin Chief Malatchee. Although women at that time were not eligible to own property in

Juliette Gordon Low

Juliette Gordon (1860–1927) was born into a prominent family in Savannah just a few months before the Civil War. She grew up surrounded by artistic and social activities. In 1886, she married William Mackay Low.

While she was traveling in England, Low met Sir Robert Baden-Powell, the founder of the Boy Scouts. She was so inspired by Sir Robert and his sister, who had formed the Girl Guides, that she returned to Georgia and, in 1912, started the Girl Scouts of America. Low committed the rest of her life to the organization she said she founded "for the purpose of helping good girls become great women." ■

Georgia, the courts recognized Mary as the legal owner of the islands. In 1866, Georgia became the first state to pass legislation allowing women to have full property rights.

Other opportunities—such as voting, serving in elected offices, and serving on juries—were also denied to women. In the early twentieth century, Rebecca Lattimer Felton began advocating

Georgian Women In Office

1923 Viola Ross Napier and Bessie Kempton Crowell become the first female members of the Georgia House of Representatives.

1965 Grace Towns Hamilton (right) becomes the first African-American woman to serve in the Georgia House of Representatives.

1993 Cynthia McKinney becomes the first African-American woman to represent Georgia in the U.S. House of Representatives. ■

reforms, including granting women the right to vote and to receive pay equal to what men earned for the same type of work. Felton also advocated compulsory education to improve the lives of Georgia's women.

Despite the efforts of women such as Felton and Juliette Gordon Low, Georgia was the first state to reject the Nineteenth Amendment to the Constitution, which gave women the right to vote. Enough states did ratify the amendment, however, and, in 1920, women in Georgia voted for the first time.

Winning World War II

The surprise attack by the Japanese on Pearl Harbor, Hawaii, on December 7, 1941, brought an influx of soldiers, sailors, and airmen to Georgia. Thousands of infantry soldiers were trained at Fort Stewart, Fort Gordon, and Fort Benning, now the site of the U.S. Army Infantry Museum. Fort Stewart, which covers 279,270 acres (113,104 ha) within five counties, is the largest infantry base east of the Mississippi today.

Hundreds of bombers were built in airplane factories in Marietta. Savannah dockworkers loaded more weapons bound for Europe than were shipped from any other port in the country. In less than two years, shipbuilders at Brunswick Shipyards built and launched ninety-nine of the famous Liberty ships, which carried supplies for America's European allies.

World War II (1941–1945) was the pivotal event in Georgia's economic transformation. Because of massive federal spending within the state, Georgia was no longer dependent on its agricul-

Bridge of Ships

At the beginning of World War II, President Franklin Delano Roosevelt promised to build a "bridge of ships" from the United States to its European allies. Each of the cargo-carrying ships, known as Liberty ships, was 447 feet (136 m) in length, required 3,425 tons of hull steel, and required 592,000 hours of labor to build.

The average construction time, from start to completion, was sixty days. On one occasion, however, the navy informed the Brunswick Shipyard workers that it would need six ships in one month. The workers guaranteed they would deliver seven. All seven ships were delivered as promised— including one that was completely built in less than five days. ■

ture economy. In 1941, a new military installation was built near Macon. It is now Warner Robins Air Force Base and Warner Robins Air Logistics Center, which together cover 8,790 acres (3,560 ha) and are the state's largest employer.

Battles after the War

The end of World War II brought opportunity, new industries, and better methods of farming to Georgia, but the state's racial problems intensified. The civil rights movement gained power as explosive battles were waged to force the integration of Georgia's public schools. Other battles were fought to overturn Georgia's unjust voting laws. It would take more than one man to solve all these problems, but one man would show how it could be done—Dr. Martin Luther King Jr.

Dr. Martin Luther King Jr.

Martin Luther King Jr. was born in Atlanta on January 15, 1929. Like his father, he became a Baptist preacher. He earned degrees from Morehouse College and Crozer Theological Seminary, then earned a doctorate at Boston University. King began advocating nonviolent desegregation while he was pastor of the Dexter Avenue Baptist Church in Montgomery, Alabama. In 1957, he founded the Southern Christian Leadership Conference.

The first attempt to integrate schools in Albany, Georgia, turned into a violent confrontation, and King stepped forward to try to resolve the issue. In doing so, he stepped into the leadership

Martin Luther King Jr. in Washington, D.C., in August 1963

role that many believe he was destined to assume—not only in Georgia's history, but in the history of the world.

On August 28, 1963, King delivered his famous speech, "I Have a Dream," before 250,000 people who had gathered in Washington, D.C., to support federal civil rights legislation. In 1964, he was awarded the Nobel Prize for his work as the leader of the modern civil rights movement. King was the youngest person and the only Georgian ever to receive the international award.

The Martin Luther King Jr. Center for Nonviolent Change in Atlanta

King lived to see part of his dream come true when the Civil Rights Act of 1964 was passed. This act protected the rights of every person to have equal access to public facilities and public education, regardless of that person's race. King also saw the passage of the Voting Rights Act of 1965, which ensured that no racial barrier would prevent a person from being able to vote.

King's leadership role in the civil rights movement made him one of the best-known Georgians of the twentieth century, but it also cost him his life. On April 4, 1968, he was assassinated by James Earl Ray.

King is buried at the Martin Luther King Jr. Center for Nonviolent Social Change in Atlanta. Perhaps nothing more eloquently expresses the enduring impact of Dr. King on Georgia and the world than the slogan for the 1996 Summer Centennial Olympics: "Atlanta, Come Celebrate the Dream."

"I Have a Dream": An Excerpt from Dr. Martin Luther King Jr.'s Speech

I say to you today, my friends, that in spite of the difficulties and frustrations of the moment, I still have a dream. It is a dream deeply rooted in the American dream. I have a dream that one day this nation will rise up and live out the true meaning of its creed: "We hold these truths to be self-evident: that all men are created equal."

I have a dream that one day on the red hills of Georgia the sons of former slaves and the sons of former slaveowners will be able to sit down together at a table of brotherhood. ■

CHAPTER FIVE

Natural Georgia

Autumn in the Georgia mountains

Georgia is a natural beauty. The 58,910 square miles (152,577 sq km) that make up the largest state east of the Mississippi River has been likened to a large apron: a ring of mountains (the southern Appalachians) at its neck, a wide waistband of forests and farms (the central Piedmont Plateau) across its middle, and a skirt of swamps and seacoasts (the coastal plain) with ruffles (the barrier islands) along the edge. The apron strings are the Savannah River, forming the border with South Carolina to the east, and the Chattahoochee River, separating Georgia from Alabama on the west.

The rugged north terrain of Georgia's Appalachian Mountain range includes the Blue Ridge and Cohutta Mountains, which are part of the Smoky Mountain range. The highest point in Georgia is Mount Enotah at 4,784 feet (1,459 m). It is also known as Brasstown Bald because its grassy crest is surrounded by the tall forests of the 38,000-acre (15,390-ha) Cohutta Wilderness Area, which spreads across the Georgia-Tennessee border. From the divide of the Blue Ridge Mountains, water runs either to the Atlantic Ocean via the Savannah River or to the Gulf of Mexico via the Chattahoochee or Tennessee Rivers.

Soil and Sand

The Piedmont Plateau at the foot of the Appalachian Mountains comprises 30 percent of the state. Iron-rich clay soils turn to rich,

Opposite: Dawn on Jekyll Island

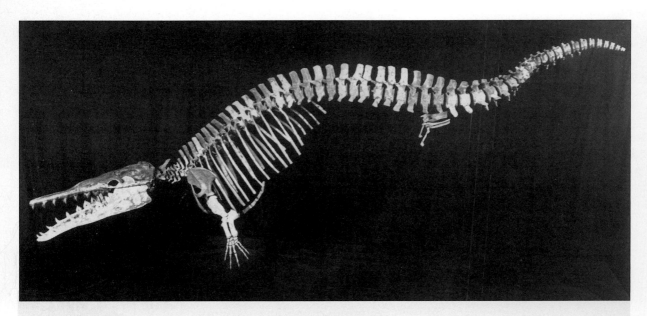

Colossal Fossil

Millions of years ago, the present-day cities of Augusta, Macon, and Columbus were underwater. This ancient coastline, now along the southern boundary of the Piedmont Plateau, is known as the Fall Line.

In 1973, the remains of a 40-million-year-old whale skeleton were discovered about 10 miles (16 km) from Macon. The fossil was 60 percent intact. Today, it is on display at Macon's Museum of Arts and Sciences. ■

dark earth as the rolling hills of the plateau smooth out into the lowlands of the coastal plain region, which covers the southern half of the state. These soils sustain Georgia's role as a world leader in crop production.

More than 100 million years of soil erosion produced a large gash south of Columbus in Stewart County. Georgians refer to it as the Little Grand Canyon. In southeastern Georgia, sandy soils and sand dunes along the Flint River south of Albany are a reminder of the state's ancient history as a seabed.

Lake Sidney Lanier

Water Wonders

Throughout Georgia, there are more than 20 lakes of at least 500 acres (202.5 ha), more than 4,000 miles (6,436 km) of freshwater rivers, and thousands of smaller ponds. Carters Lake, formed when the Coosa River was dammed, is 465 feet (142 m) deep—the deepest lake east of the Mississippi River.

Dams built along the Chatta-hoochee River have created two of the state's most popular attractions: Lake Seminole and Lake Sidney Lanier. Anglers cast for freshwater trout, bream, pike, black bass, catfish, red-fish, and drum. Ocean fishing includes sea trout, flounder, shrimp, crab, and various species of shark.

North Georgia is famous for its waterfalls, known as cataracts. Toc-coa, Amicalola, and Tallulah Falls are

Georgia's topography

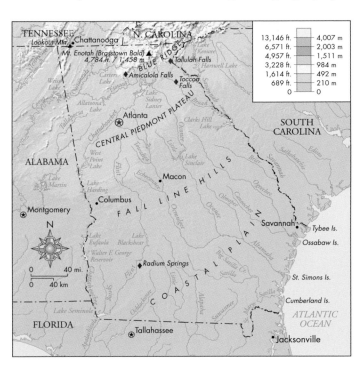

Toccoa Falls, one of Georgia's most compelling sights

among the best-known falling-water sites in the state. Toccoa Falls is 19 feet (5.8 m) higher than New York's Niagara Falls. Amicalola is the highest waterfall east of the Mississippi River. Tallulah Falls thunders through Tallulah Gorge, the nation's oldest natural gorge. The gorge is 3 miles (4.8 km) wide and 1,200 feet (366 m) deep.

You can't see most of the water in Georgia. The Floridan Aquifer under the southwest part of the state is one of the largest underground water supplies in North America. Its limestone reservoirs hold millions of gallons of water, collected from Georgia's annual average rainfall of more than 50 inches (130 cm). Since 1975, the number of acres irrigated by the aquifer has increased; Decatur County leads the state with 89,000 irrigated acres (36,045 ha).

Radium Springs in Dougherty County is the largest natural spring in Georgia. Every minute, 70,000 gallons (264,950 l) of water flow from Radium Springs.

Tops in Trees

"You can't have trees without Georgia, or Georgia without trees!" reads a sign in Georgia's Dixie Memorial State Forest. Two national forests, the Chattahoochee in northern Georgia and the Oconee in central Georgia, cover almost 1 million acres (405,000 ha). Georgia has 24 million forested acres (9.7 million ha) covered with pine,

Lanier Land

Sidney Clopton Lanier (1842–1881) was born in Macon. His fascination for romantic writers and his love of nature, acquired while growing up in rural Georgia, led him to a career as a poet and novelist. He was also a gifted musician.

Lanier served with the Macon Volunteers during the Civil War and spent a year as a Union prisoner of war. While he was imprisoned, he contracted tuberculosis. His first novel, *Tiger-Lilies,* was based on his wartime experiences. His most famous poems, "Song of the Chattahoochee" and "The Marshes of Glynn." Other sites in Georgia named in his honor include Lanier County, Lanier Islands, Lake Sidney Lanier, and the Lanier Covered Bridge in Glynn County. ■

Georgia's Geographical Features

Total area; rank	58,977 sq. mi. (152,750 sq km); 24th
Land; rank	57,919 sq. mi. (150,010 sq km); 21st
Water; rank	1,058 sq. mi. (2,740 sq km); 28th
Inland water; rank	1,011 sq. mi. (2,618 sq km); 20th
Coastal water; rank	47 sq. mi. (122 sq km); 18th
Geographic center	Twiggs, 18 miles (29 km) southeast of Macon
Highest point	Brasstown Bald Mountain, 4,784 feet (1,458 m)
Lowest point	Sea level at the Atlantic Ocean
Largest city	Atlanta
Longest river	Savannah River, 350 miles (563 km)
Population; rank	6,508,419 (1990 census); 11th
Record high temperature	113°F (45°C) at Greenville on May 27, 1978
Record low temperature	−17°F (−27°C) at Floyd County on January 27, 1940
Average July temperature	80°F (27°C)
Average January temperature	47°F (8°C)
Average annual precipitation	50 inches (127 cm)

Georgia-Pacific Group

Georgia-Pacific Group, headquartered in Atlanta, is the top U.S. manufacturer, distributor, and wholesaler of building products, including lumber, siding, doors, and drywall. It is also one of the leading producers of paper products, such as bathroom tissue, paper towels, and envelopes. The company employs 47,000 workers; in 1996, its gross sales were almost $13 million.

The Timber Company is a division of Georgia-Pacific Group. It is the third-largest private timberland holder in North America. The Timber Company owns approximately 5.4 million acres (2.2 million ha) of timberland in the United States and Canada. Nearly one million acres (405,000 ha) are in Georgia. ■

The national champion cabbage palmetto in Brunswick

cedar, oak, elm, sycamore, poplar, palm, red maple, cypress, willow, hickory, gum, hemlock, dogwood, and magnolia (the most famous of Georgia's flowering trees).

In 1991, a cabbage palmetto in Brunswick was named a national champion on the American Forests' National Register of Big Trees, which cites the largest known tree of each native and naturalized species in the continental United States. The winning tree, a member of the palm family, stands 62 feet (19 m) tall.

American forestry officials report that there are more seedling trees planted in rural areas in Georgia than in any other state in the nation. Pine are the most predominant. Slash and longleaf pines produce gums that are made into turpentine, tar, and pitch. Loblolly, shortleaf, slash, and longleaf pines are used for lumber and pulp.

Smell the Flowers

The smell of magnolia blossoms is not the only fragrance for which Georgia is well known. The scents of dogwood, peach, apple, and cherry blossoms are frequently in the air. Honeysuckle, gardenia, and wisteria blend their colors and fragrances with azalea, snapdragon, larkspur, rhododendron, mountain laurel, and more than 1,400 other species of flowers and shrubs.

In the Appalachians of northeast Georgia, fields filled with sunflowers and green cinnamon fern share the landscape. Ginseng, a plant that produces a root valued for its medicinal purposes, grows wild in this area. Herbal tonics and teas made from wild ginseng leaves have been touted in Blue Ridge folklore and are still prized for their curative powers.

Dogwoods are among Georgia's many flowering trees.

Keep Off the Grass

Wire grass, cordgrass, and sea oats are the predominant grasses of Georgia. Eighteenth-century naturalist William Bartram was particularly intrigued by the wiry stalks of the wire grass he found throughout the pine barren regions. The Georgia Department of Transportation has designated State Highway 57, a 70-mile (113-km) road between Interstate 16 and Interstate 95 in south-

Kudzu Calamity

In the early 1930s, Georgia farmers were paid $5 an acre (0.4 ha) to plant a tough, protein-rich vine called kudzu to stop soil erosion. Kudzu Klubs were formed to promote the vine to city residents as well as farmers. Unfortunately, the vine thrived in Georgia's soil and climate so well that it became a climbing monster.

Kudzu is such a hardy plant that it takes over everything—from fields to front porches—choking every other plant in its path, invading waterways, and even pulling down utility poles and destroying buildings. Thousands of acres of kudzu now cover Georgia, and there's still no way to stop it from spreading. ■

east Georgia, as the Wiregrass Trail. It is also known as Bartram's Corridor.

Marshland cordgrass is a familiar sight in the coastal areas. The sea oats growing on the beaches are so critical to preserving the environment that the grass is protected by law.

Endangered Efforts

In 1985, Georgia became the first state to allow taxpayers to designate a portion of their state-tax refunds to provide additional money for the its department of natural resources. The department manages, protects, and preserves Georgia's 930 animal and 3,600 plant species.

Georgia was also among the first states in the nation to pass legislation protecting its tidal marshlands. Most of north Georgia's Appalachian woodlands are under the protection of the 749,000-acre (303,345-ha) Chattahoochee National Forest.

Above the Fall Line (from Augusta to Columbus), you can hike through Oconee National Forest and the 35,000-acre

Georgia's coastal sea oats, which help preserve the sand dunes, are protected by law.

William Bartram

William Bartram (1739–1823) first traveled to Georgia in 1765 with his father, John Bartram, who had been appointed Botanist Royal in America by King George III. In 1773, William, an accomplished naturalist and artist, returned to research the plant, bird, and animal life of the region. In 1791, he published his book *Travels through North and South Carolina, Georgia, East and West Florida*.

Bartram's journey from the northeast corner of Georgia to Augusta and the Savannah River is now called the Bartram Trail. The 220-mile (354-km) trail passes over Rabun Bald, the second tallest peak in Georgia. Only a 37-mile (60-km) stretch of the trail is maintained for hikers. Volunteer workers under the direction of conservation groups attempt to keep the rest of the trail marked. Bartram explored more of North America than any scientist of his time and is considered America's first naturalist. ■

(14,175-ha) Piedmont National Wildlife Refuge. During May and June, more than forty colonies of endangered red-cockaded woodpeckers make their nests inside the pine trees of the refuge. These birds had almost disappeared from Georgia before they were given this protected area in which to live. Other birds in danger of extinction—throughout all or parts of their ranges in Georgia—are the ivory-billed woodpecker, Kirtland's warbler, the peregrine falcon, the wood stork, and Bachman's warbler.

Only about 350 right whales are known to exist in the world. The right whale calves off the Georgia coast top the list of mammals identified as endangered by the Georgia Department of Natural Resources. Also on the list are the Florida panther, eastern

The Chattahoochee National Forest provides protection for north Georgia's Appalachian woodlands.

Gentle Giants of Georgia

Endangered manatees live in the coastal waters of Georgia. They love to eat the cordgrass found in the salt marshes. Adult manatees weighing as much as 3,000 pounds (1,362 kg) consume 100 pounds (45 kg) of food a day. They push their food into their mouths with their flippers, which makes them slow swimmers while they are eating.

Warnings are posted for pleasure boaters to watch out for these gentle giants. There are only about 1,500 manatees living in the wild in the United States. ■

cougar, humpback whale, gray bat, Indiana bat, and West Indian manatee.

Reptiles in danger of extinction throughout all or part of Georgia include the leatherneck sea turtle, hawksbill sea turtle, and Kemp's ridley sea turtle. Among the endangered fish are the Altamaha shiner, lipstick darter, stippled starfish, flame chub, frecklebelly madtom, and fatlips minnow.

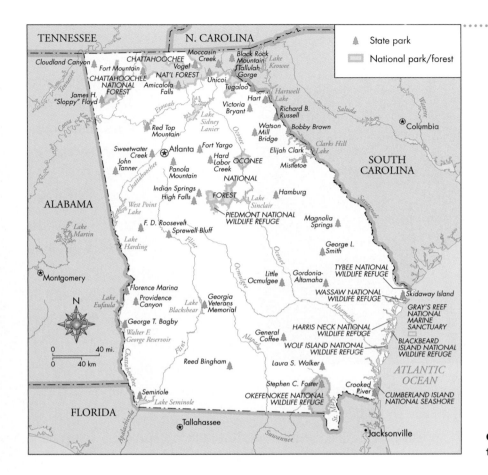

Georgia's parks and forests

Swamp Sights

To a bald eagle circling overhead, the Okefenokee Swamp might look like a giant saucer filled with brown tea. The Seminole Indian name for this murky bog means "Land of Trembling Earth." The gases escaping from the rotting trees and plants make the 15-foot (4.6-m)-thick swamp floor quiver. Moss-covered cypress trees and pines keep the swamp dark, even on a bright summer day.

This "saucer swamp" was once part of the ocean floor. It is one of the oldest freshwater ecosystems in the United States. It extends approximately 38 miles (61 km) from north to south and 25 miles

The Okefenokee National Wildlife Refuge is home to many species of birds, reptiles, and mammals.

(40 km) east to west. No roads cross the Okefenokee. Wood snakes, black bears, and alligators are some of the creatures living in this swamp.

The Okefenokee National Wildlife Refuge is home to more than 230 species of birds, 50 species of reptiles, and 40 species of mammals. Several of its residents are on the federal Endangered Species List. Thousands of plant species— some barely large enough to see without a microscope—are also listed as endangered.

Visitors can take a guided boat tour at Okefenokee Swamp Park in Waycross or at the Suwannee Canal Recreation Area at Folkston. Campers at Stephen Foster State Park at Fargo canoe the swamp early in the morning, when flying squirrels are most likely to be seen. Explorers should always keep an eye out for one of the 12,000 alligators who live in the swamp.

Chemical Concerns

Titanium ore has been discovered near Okefenokee Swamp on land that is owned by a chemical-manufacturing corporation. The ore is not found anywhere else in the United States. Titanium is a lightweight, silver-gray metal used to build structures with enormous strength. Titanium ore is also used to make titanium dioxide—a white pigment used in everything from hospital gloves and plastic forks to the letter *m* on M&M candies.

The chemical company is working closely with all those responsible for preserving the Okefenokee. The company believes it can mine the ore without causing any damage to the swamp or its residents. Some people, however, are concerned that the smoke and noise surrounding the mining operation would be harmful to the lifes-forms in the swamp.

Barrier Buffers

The Okefenokee isn't the only wildlife refuge in Georgia. The islands along the coast of the Atlantic Ocean provide 55,000 acres (22,275 ha) of sanctuaries for migratory birds, sea turtles, and wild horses. The horses are descendants of those left by Spanish missionaries in the late seventeenth century.

Wassaw National Wildlife Refuge, Wolf Island National Wildlife Refuge, Savannah National Wildlife Refuge, and Tybee National Wildlife Refuge are located on Georgia's barrier islands. Harris Neck National Wildlife Refuge is located on land that was a U.S. Army airfield during World War II. Cumberland Island National Seashore, which can only be reached by boat, allows no more than 300 visitors ashore each day.

The Cumberland Island National Seashore can only be reached by boat.

Wild Weather

Georgia has its share of wild weather. Record temperatures range from a low of –17° F (–27° C) recorded on January 27, 1940, to a high of 113° F (45° C) recorded on May 27, 1978.

Tropical storms and hurricanes have a serious impact on Georgia, but tornadoes and floods are responsible for the state's worst natural disasters. In 1903, a tornado killed 203 people in Gainesville. In 1936, the town was struck by another tornado, which killed 187 people.

The Flint River Flood 31 people in 1994. The river had not flooded since 1925. Water covered an area the size of Rhode Island and Massachusetts combined. Thousands of livestock and poultry also drowned. Georgia's largest commercial catfish farm in Baker County had more than one million catfish washed out of the farm ponds.

Demon Drought, Fickle Flood

Georgia is a state of extremes. The year after a flood, it may not rain enough—and the same area that was underwater one year might become a drought disaster area the next. For example, in 1997, the lack of rain in southwest Georgia meant disaster for farmers. Half of the crops in thirteen counties were lost. Earlier in the year, these same counties had been damaged by Hurricane Danny.

Georgia experiences three types of floods: river floods, coastal floods, and flash floods. River floods occur when rains, sometimes coupled with melting snow, fill the river basins with too much water too quickly. In some locations, torrential rains from decaying hurricanes or tropical systems can also cause river flooding. Coastal floods occur when winds generated from tropical storms and hurricanes drive water inland. Flash floods are usually due to enormous amounts of rain falling in a short period of time. Flash flooding accounts for the majority of flood deaths in Georgia.

Tornadoes are violent rotating columns of air with winds of more than 200 miles per hour (322 kph). The average diameter of a Georgia tornado is 1,000 feet (305 m), with an average forward speed of 30 miles per hour (48 kph). Tornadoes are the most frequent and the most destructive of Georgia's weather phenomena.

Tornadoes have caused severe damage in the state of Georgia.

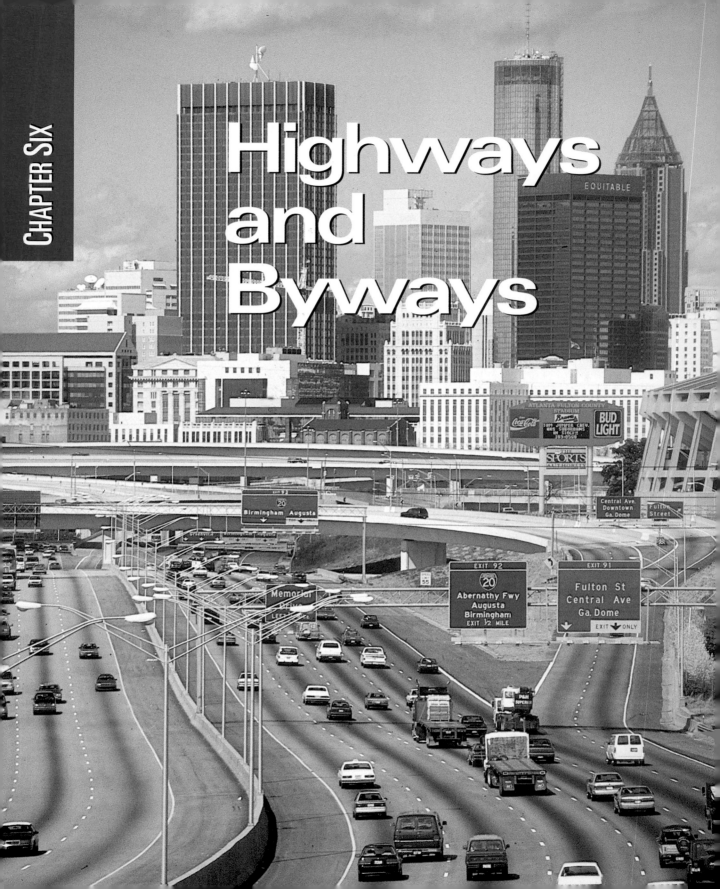

CHAPTER SIX

Highways and Byways

More than 110,000 miles (176,990 km) of modern highways and quiet byways will take you almost anywhere in Georgia that you want to go. Rivers play a significant role in Georgia's transportation system, too, and there are 250 airports in addition to Hartsfield International.

The Cotton Exchange Museum in Augusta

No matter which type of transportation you take, the most important thing is to take your time. "Georgia is a friend you love saying hello to," reads a billboard on Interstate 95 near Valdosta. Actually, the nine distinct regions of Georgia are nine "friends" who will make you feel right at home any time you stop by to visit. The nine regions of Georgia are the Classic South, Colonial Coast, Historic Heartland, Magnolia Midlands, Northeast Georgia Mountains, Northwest Georgia Mountains, Plantation Trace, and Presidential Pathways.

The Classic South

The region in east-central Georgia known as the Classic South is bordered by the Piedmont Plateau to the north and the Atlantic Coastal Plain to the south. The historic city of Augusta is located in this region.

Augusta was founded as a trading post by James Oglethorpe in

Opposite: Roads leading into Atlanta

Ware's Folly

In 1818, Nicholas Ware spent the then astounding sum of $40,000 to build a house in Augusta. Because of the cost, some called the house Ware's Folly.

In 1819, Ware became mayor of Augusta and, in 1821, he became a U.S. senator. The Gertrude Herbert Memorial Institute of Art is housed in the former Ware mansion. ■

1735. During the nineteenth century, fortunes were made in the city as brokers spent their days buying and selling at the Cotton Exchange Building. Today, the Victorian structure, built on the Savannah River in 1886, houses the Cotton Exchange Museum. Good fortune is still a part of life in Augusta—where the richest drag boat race in the world is held each year and the Masters Tournament brings together the best golfers in the world to compete each spring.

You may have already seen Crawfordville but just didn't know it. This city is a favorite location for filmmakers and television producers. Alexander H. Stephens State Historic Park, named to honor the former Confederate vice president (1861–1865) and governor of Georgia (1882–1883), is a favorite stop of Civil War buffs. Within the park is Stephens's home, Liberty Hall, built around 1875, and the Confederate Museum, which houses one of the finest collections of Confederate artifacts in Georgia.

The area surrounding Lake Oconee, near Milledgeville, was a favorite hunting ground for Cherokee and Creek Indians. Lake Oconee is the second-largest lake in Georgia.

If you have ever had a stomachache, you have probably been helped by kaolin, a product produced in Sandersville. Made from

Alexander Hamilton Stephens

Alexander Hamilton Stephens (1812–1883) was born near Crawfordville. He served in the Georgia House of Representatives (1837–1841), the state senate (1842–1843), and in the U.S. House of Representatives (1843–1859). Although he did not favor Georgia's leaving the Union, Stephens left his seat in the U.S. Congress when Georgia seceded. In 1861, he was elected vice president of the Confederate States of America.

After the Civil War ended in 1865, Stephens remained a popular politician in Georgia. He ran for several offices. He was never defeated in any election. He died in 1883, while serving as governor of Georgia. ■

white clay, kaolin is used in medicines, eye shadow, and plastics. It is one of Georgia's largest exports. The Kaolin Festival held each October is just one of the area's favorite annual festivals. The Georgia Field Trials, one of the nation's oldest hunting-dog competitions, is held in Waynesboro, the Bird Dog Capital of the World.

Rumor has it that when General Robert E. Lee fled the Union army, he hid the South's gold on Chennault Plantation in Lincolnton. Some people claim that the ghosts of Confederate and Union soldiers still come looking for it on stormy nights.

The Colonial Coast

The Colonial Coast region of Georgia breezes along at a gentle pace. If you don't want to visit Savannah's more than 1,000 historic buildings, you can take a carriage ride through the twenty-two garden squares, or get a lesson in maritime history at the Ships of the Sea Museum.

Tybee Island is the northernmost of Georgia's thirteen barrier islands, which are known as the Golden Isles. The 80 miles

Some of Savannah's beautiful, restored historic homes

(129 km) separating Savannah from the islands can be traveled quickly on Interstate 95, but you will want to take time to explore the small towns along the route. Darien is Georgia's second-oldest town. From Darien, you can ride the ferry to Sapelo Island, which was once the center of tobacco king R. J. Reynolds's personal empire.

After the Revolutionary War, some of the sea islands became cotton plantations. After the Civil War, these plantations were mostly left in ruins. In 1886, some of America's wealthiest men purchased Jekyll Island and built an elegant private resort there. In 1947, the state bought back Jekyll Island, so now everyone can enjoy this public recreation facility.

St. Simons Island was home to writer Eugenia Price. Missionary brothers John and Charles Wesley built their first church there in 1736.

John and Charles Wesley

John (1703–1791) and Charles (1707–1788) Wesley were born in England. The brothers were two of fifteen children born to Susanna and Samuel Wesley. John became a preacher. Charles wrote hymns.

In 1735, the two men traveled to Georgia as missionaries but felt that their efforts to convert the Indians failed. They returned to England where their fervent religious beliefs helped inspire a new denomination within the Church of England, known as the Methodists. ▪

Georgia's cities and interstates

Shrimp fishing is an important industry for Georgia.

St. Marys Historic District is the only historic district in America with signage for the blind. Don't leave this part of the "low country" without enjoying a shrimp feast in Brunswick, where thousands of visitors come to support the city's claim as Shrimp Capital of the World.

Some of the region, including the Okefenokee Swamp, can only be explored by boat. Swamp lore and folktales, including stories of Obediah Barber (1825–1909), King of the Okefenok, are favorite stories in Folkston and Waycross.

The Historic Heartland

Peach production and historic preservation are a big part of what goes on in the Historic Heartland in the central part of Georgia. The Peach Blossom Trail stretches along U.S. Highways 341 and 41 from Jonesboro and McDonough south to Forsyth, Fort Valley, and Perry. Perry is also the home of the Georgia National Fairgrounds and Agricenter. Some folks call it "the city of blossoms and broncs."

Peaches are plentiful in Perry, and so are the signs urging you to "Pick Your Own." The signs do not apply, however, to the 9 acres (3.6 ha) of pink and white camellias at Massee Lane Gardens, the American Camellia Society's headquarters in nearby Fort Valley. Massee Lane is also known nationally for its beautiful porcelain collection, which is on display in the Stevens-Taylor Gallery Building and in the Annabelle Lundy Fetterman Educational Museum.

The 117-mile (188-km) Antebellum Trail runs through the historic towns of Athens, Watkinsville, Madison, Eatonton, Milledgeville, and Macon. Graceful southern architecture fills the towns along the trail. Among the jewels in Georgia's crown of classic structures are the Taylor-Grady House in Athens, the Old Governor's Mansion in Milledgeville, and the Hay House in Macon. The cemeteries in Milledgeville contain interesting examples of the South's unique culture and customs.

Athens is the home of the University of Georgia and the Georgia Museum of Art. The exhibits in Butts-Mehre Heritage Hall Sports Museum tell of the achievements of Georgia's athletes and teams. Other museums and historic sites include the Museum of Aviation at Robins Air Force Base and the Uncle Remus Museum

Peach Pie

Ingredients:

  8 large ripe peaches, peeled, pitted,
     and cut into 1-inch slices
1/2 cup sugar
1/4 cup all-purpose flour
     juice of half a lemon
  2 9-inch unbaked pie shells
     flour
     milk

Directions:

Preheat oven to 375°F.

In a large bowl, combine peaches, sugar, flour, and lemon juice. Pour filling into one of the pie shells.

Powder a surface and a rolling pin with flour, and roll the second pie shell flat. Cut the shell into 1-inch thick slices, and arrange the slices in a lattice over the pie filling. Trim away any of the slices that hang over the side of the pie. Seal the lattice strips to the pie shell by dampening the edge of the shell with water and gently pressing the strips into it.

Brush the lattice with milk, and bake for 50 minutes or until the crust has turned a golden brown and the filling is bubbling.

in Eatonton, which centers on the beloved Uncle Remus tales of Georgia author Joel Chandler Harris.

Macon is the largest city in the Historic Heartland. Among its many outstanding attractions are the Georgia Music Hall of Fame; the Museum of Arts and Sciences, which has one of the largest planetariums in the state; and the Tubman African American Museum, named for abolitionist Harriet Tubman, who helped slaves escape through the Underground Railroad.

In the Pink

The city planners of Macon, inspired by the ancient Hanging Gardens of Babylon, planted hundreds of Yoshino cherry trees. Today, Macon displays more than 150,000 cherry trees. Each spring, visitors enjoy the city's hospitality during the Macon Cherry Blossom Festival. ■

The Magnolia Midlands

The scent of magnolia blossoms is only one of the delightful aromas in the Magnolia Midlands. In March, you will catch a whiff of the Claxton Fruit Cake Festival. In May, you'll be tantalized by the pungent smells of the Vidalia Sweet Onion Festival. The world's best pecan log rolls are made in Eastman every day by the Stuckey's Candy Company, and the scent will stay with you long after you leave town.

Be sure to visit the town of Alma, home of the Georgia Blueberry Festival, and General Coffee State Park in Douglas, named for General John Coffee (1772–1833), a planter, U.S. congressman, and military leader.

Statesboro is the home of Georgia Southern University (GSU), and the university's museum is the home of a 78-million-year-old Mosasaur fossil. After you leave GSU and the Age of Dinosaurs, tour the high-tech world of nuclear power at the Hatch Nuclear Plant in Baxley.

The Northeast Georgia Mountains

Gainesville is the largest city in the eighteen-county region of the Northeast Georgia Mountains—and it is filled with places in which to enjoy the outdoors. Take your time touring the Elachee Nature Science Center. You will find plenty of racing thrills at Road Atlanta Motorsports Complex between Braselton and Gainesville.

White-water rafting on the Chattahoochee River

The Russell-Brasstown Scenic Byway is a 38-mile (61-km) loop just north of the scenic village of Helen. It is one of two routes in Georgia designated as scenic byways by the U.S. Forest Service. This is Georgia's waterfall country, so remember to watch for falling water along the way.

The Chattooga River runs for 40 miles (64 km) between Georgia and South Carolina. In 1974, it was designated a Wild and Scenic River. It is a favorite attraction for white-water rafters.

Miners poured into Dahlonega, "going for the gold" in the Northeast Georgia Mountains. In 1828, Benjamin Parks stubbed his toe on a nugget there and started the first gold rush in the United States. You can still pan for riches in the town, whose name means "gold" in Cherokee. So much gold was mined in Lumpkin County that a U.S. mint was built in Dahlonega, although it closed during the Civil War and later burned. North Georgia College, the nation's only four-year, coeducational, military liberal-arts college, sits on the site of the mint. The Dahlonega Courthouse Gold Museum is housed in the brick building that served as the county courthouse from 1836 to 1965.

Cleveland's Cabbage Patch

On December 19, 1823, Georgia became the first state to register birth dates. County clerks were required to enter the birth dates of their county's citizens in a record book.

In 1978, Cleveland, Georgia, recorded the first "birth" of a Cabbage Patch doll. More than 4,000 visitors a year visit Cleveland to tour Babyland General Hospital and adopt one of the popular hand-stitched dolls created by Xavier Roberts. ■

Georgia's northeast mountains are full of unique festivals and events, including Gold Rush Days in Dahlonega, the Sorghum Festival in Blairsville, Mule Camp Market in Gainesville, Mountain Laurel Festival in Clarkesville, and the Rhododendron Festival in Hiawassee.

The Northwest Georgia Mountains

"Up-country" is the way Georgians in the Northwest Georgia Mountains region refer to their part of the state. Legend has it that Cherokee Indians came to the Northwest Georgia Mountains to dance with the eagles and "created thunder in the ground." On the Chiefton's Trail at Chatsworth, the Cherokee rose "blooms" year-round on the house that Chief Vann of the Cherokees built in 1804. Vann ordered artisans to carve the delicate flower into the wood moldings of the house, the showplace of the Cherokee Nation.

New Echota was the capital of the Cherokee Nation. The inven-

Sequoyah

Sequoyah (c. 1760–1843) was born in Tennessee. His mother, Wut-teh, was Cherokee, and the man believed to be his father, Nathaniel Gist, was a Virginia fur trader. Sequoyah is also known as George Gist or George Guess (a variation of the last name).

Sequoyah never learned to speak, read, or write English, but he recognized the power of written language. He created the first syllabary, or alphabet, of the Cherokee language, which until that time was only a spoken language. The syllabary consisted of eighty-six syllables, or "talking leaves," for each spoken sound. In 1821, the Cherokee Nation adopted Sequoyah's "talking leaves" as their alphabet. By the time Sequoyah died in Mexico, thousands of Cherokees could read and write their own language. ■

tion of the Cherokee alphabet by Sequoyah in 1821 resulted in a bilingual newspaper, the *Cherokee Phoenix*, which was published in 1828 in New Echota and distributed throughout the Cherokee territory.

The Blue and Gray Trail extends 130 miles (209 km) from Chattanooga, Tennessee, to Atlanta, Georgia. The trail passes through more than fifty Civil War sites, including Chickamauga-Chattanooga National Military Park, the largest and oldest military park in the United States. The Creek Indians called this area "River of Death," referring to the malaria and other waterborne diseases that plagued their people. They had no idea how prophetic they were: During the Civil War, some 34,000 Americans were killed there in a battle that lasted only two days.

The town of Cave Springs boasts ninety stately homes that are listed on the National Register of Historic Places. Woodlands Plantation in nearby Adairsville offers a view of one of Georgia's most beautiful gardens—but for a view of northwest Georgia you can't get anywhere else, take a hang-glider flight from Lookout Mountain Flight Park.

Plantation Trace

They say the groundhog has never seen his shadow in Plantation Trace. The climate is gentle year-round in this lush section of southwest Georgia, and many plantations were built here, which is how the region got its name.

Pebble Hill Plantation, which was built by Thomas Jefferson Johnson in the 1820s

Thomas Jefferson Johnson built Pebble Hill Plantation here in the 1820s. In the late 1970s, Pansy Poe, the last owner of Pebble Hill, willed the elegant mansion to the public. Today, visitors can enjoy the artwork and other treasures that fill the house and tour the ponds, gardens, and stables on the grounds. A Grand Plantation Ball is held each spring.

Thomasville, known as the City of Roses, is said to have more roses than people. It was the favorite winter residence of wealthy northerners who flocked to the town in the nineteenth century. Stay on U.S. Highway 319 to Moultrie, where the Sunbelt Expo, the largest farm show in the southeast, is held. People come from all over the world to see the show, then head for one of the nearby quail-hunting plantations. Or, if they have Scottish ancestors, they may go to Odom Genealogy Library to research their family's roots.

Albany, the largest city in Plantation Trace, is the home of the Chehaw Wild Animal Park, a 293-acre (119-ha) wildlife preserve designed by famed naturalist Jim Fowler. Albany is also pecan-growing country, and the restaurants there are famous for their pecan specialties.

If you have never attended a cane-grinding party, you should visit the Georgia Agrirama in Tifton. The Agrirama is a living-history museum documenting life in the early nineteenth century. Southwest Georgia may hold the record for unusual fun festivities, which include the Mayhaw Festival in Colquitt, the Peanut Plantin' Pickin' Phestival in Dawson, the Hahira Honey Bee Festival, and Gnat Days in Camilla.

Valdosta is a shopper's heaven with its hundreds of outlet stores and markets. A visit to the Lowndes County Historical Society and

Population of Georgia's Major Cities (1990)	
Atlanta	394,017
Columbus	179,278
Savannah	137,560
Macon	106,612
Albany	78,122

Museum takes visitors back to the days when merchants came from all over to barter for sea-island cotton.

The Presidential Pathways

Cordele, the Watermelon Capital of the World, is a good place to begin a visit to the twenty-one-county area that presidents Franklin Delano Roosevelt and Jimmy Carter called home. Then head on up to Vienna for the annual Big Pig Jig, Georgia's official barbecue cooking championship. Nearby Macon County is the heart of Mennonite country, where visitors can experience the culture and heritage of some of Georgia's first settlers.

Aviator Charles Lindbergh made his first solo flight from the town of Americus in 1923. A few miles west is Plains, the home-town of Jimmy Carter, the thirty-ninth president of the United States. Providence Canyon, 25 miles (40 km) from Plains, has the highest concentration of wildflowers in Georgia. The plumleaf azalea is found only in the Presidential Path-ways region.

Westville is a lively historic village of the 1850s recreated at Lumpkin. Just 35 miles (56 km) to the southeast is

A farmer and his crop in Cordele, known as the Watermelon Capital of the World

Columbus, the second-largest city in Georgia. Columbus is known as the City of Fountains and also as Georgia's "West Coast" city. Among its favorite attractions is the Confederate Naval Museum, the only museum of its kind in the world, which contains the remains of two Confederate gunboats.

North of Columbus is Warm Springs. The downtown area has been restored to look much as it did during the 1920s when President Franklin Delano Roosevelt traveled there by train. Roosevelt was stricken with polio in 1921. In 1927, he founded what is today the Roosevelt Warm Springs Institute for Rehabilitation, which provides various therapies for people with disabilities.

Atlanta, Georgia's largest city, offers many things to many people.

Pine Mountain is the gateway to Callaway Gardens, a resort featuring 700 varieties of azaleas, the world's largest display of hollies, and more than 1,000 butterflies living in the largest glass-enclosed conservatory in the world. Between Pine Mountain and Atlanta, there are great places to fish. Enjoy the scenery along Chattahoochee-Flint Heritage Highway. If you are looking for a telephone, you will find plenty of them at the Georgia Rural Telephone Museum in Leslie.

The Big A

Atlanta is sometimes described as being "all things to all people." Whether or not that's true, throughout its history, it certainly has been many things to many people.

Originally, the site was a Creek settlement known as Standing Peachtree. In 1837, an area in the center of the present-day city was selected to be the southern station, or terminus, of the Western & Atlantic Railroad. The location was called Terminus. "Terminus will be a good location for one tavern, a blacksmith shop, a grocery store and nothing else," predicted the railroad's engineer Stephen Long.

In 1842, Terminus became the incorporated city of Marthasville, and in 1845, the train depot was named Atlanta. On December 29, 1845, the city of Atlanta was incorporated. Today, Atlanta covers more than 100 square miles (259 sq km) and is home to almost 400,000 people.

Underground Atlanta is one of the area's best-known attractions.

CHAPTER SEVEN

The Power of the People

n 1777, Georgia adopted its first state constitution. Other state constitutions followed in 1789, 1798, 1861, 1865, 1868, 1877, 1945, and 1976. The current constitution was adopted in 1982.

Like the federal government, the government of Georgia is divided into legislative, executive, and judicial branches. The legislative branch is called the General Assembly. There are 56 state senators and 180 state representatives elected by the people to serve two-year terms. Georgia's General Assembly, the third-largest lawmaking body in the country, meets in the state capitol in Atlanta each January to begin a forty-day session.

The executive branch is headed by the governor of Georgia. The governor is elected to a four-year term and may serve only two consecutive terms. The office of lieutenant governor is different, however; he or she may serve as many terms as elected. Georgia's constitution also provides for the people to elect a secretary of state, attorney general, commissioner of agriculture, commissioner of insurance, commissioner of labor, and state school superintendent.

The judicial branch interprets the laws. Each county in Georgia has a magistrate court, probate court, and juvenile court. There are superior courts for forty-six judicial districts, sixty-four state courts, a court of appeals, and the Georgia supreme court.

The Georgia House of Representatives in session

Opposite: The state capitol

Governors of Georgia

Name	Party	Term	Name	Party	Term
John A. Treutlen	Whig	1777–1778	Charles J. Jenkins	Dem.	1865–1868
John Houstoun	Whig	1778–1779	Brig. Gen. Thomas H. Ruger	U.S. military governor	1868
John Wereat	Whig	1779–1780	Rufus B. Bullock	Rep.	1868–1871
George Walton	Whig	1779–1780	Benjamin Conley	Rep.	1871–1872
Richard Howley	Whig	1780	James M. Smith	Dem.	1872–1877
Stephen Heard	Whig	1780	Alfred H. Colquitt	Dem.	1877–1882
Myrick Davies	Whig	1780–1781	Alexander H. Stephens	Dem	1882–1883
Nathan Brownson	Whig	1781–1782	James S. Boynton	Dem.	1883
John Martin	Whig	1782–1783	Henry D. McDaniel	Dem.	1883–1886
Lyman Hall	None	1783–1784	John B. Gordon	Dem.	1886–1890
John Houstoun	None	1784–1785	William J. Northen	Dem.	1890–1894
Samuel Elbert	None	1785–1786	William Y. Atkinson	Dem.	1894–1898
Edward Telfair	None	1786–1787	Allen D. Candler	Dem.	1898–1902
George Mathews	None	1787–1788	Joseph M. Terrell	Dem.	1902–1907
George Handley	None	1788–1789	Hoke Smith	Dem.	1907–1909
George Walton	None	1789–1790	Joseph M. Brown	Dem.	1909–1911
Edward Telfair	None	1790–1793	Hoke Smith	Dem.	1911
George Mathews	None	1793–1796	John M. Slaton	Dem.	1911–1912
Jared Irwin	None	1796–1798	Joseph M. Brown	Dem.	1912–1913
James Jackson	Jeff.-Rep.*	1798–1801	John M. Slaton	Dem.	1913–1915
David Emanuel	Jeff.-Rep.*	1801	Nathaniel E. Harris	Dem.	1915–1917
Josiah Tattnall, Jr	Jeff.-Rep.*	1801–1802	Hugh M. Dorsey	Dem.	1917–1921
John Milledge	Jeff.-Rep.*	1802–1806	Thomas W. Hardwick	Dem.	1921–1923
Jared Irwin	Jeff.-Rep.*	1806–1809	Clifford Walker	Dem.	1923–1927
David B. Mitchell	Jeff.-Rep.*	1809–1813	Lamartine G. Hardman	Dem.	1927–1931
Peter Early	Jeff.-Rep.*	1813–1815	Richard B. Russell, Jr.	Dem.	1931–1933
David B. Mitchell	Jeff.-Rep.*	1815–1817	Eugene Talmadge	Dem.	1933–1937
William Rabun	Jeff.-Rep.*	1817–1819	Eurith D. Rivers	Dem.	1937–1941
Matthew Talbot	Jeff.-Rep.*	1819	Eugene Talmadge	Dem.	1941–1943
John Clark	Jeff.-Rep.*	1819–1823	Ellis Arnall	Dem.	1943–1947
George M. Troup	Jeff.-Rep.*	1823–1827	Melvin E. Thompson	Dem.	1947–1948
John Forsyth	Jeff.-Rep.*	1827–1829	Herman E. Talmadge	Dem.	1948–1955
George R. Gilmer	Whig	1829-1831	Marvin Griffin	Dem.	1955–1959
Wilson Lumpkin	Dem.	1831–1835	Ernest Vandiver	Dem.	1959–1963
William Schley	Dem.	1835–1837	Carl E. Sanders	Dem.	1963–1967
George R. Gilmer	Whig	1837–1839	Lester G. Maddox	Dem.	1967–1971
Charles J. McDonald	Dem	1839–1843	Jimmy Carter	Dem.	1971–1975
George W. Crawford	Whig	1843–1847	George D. Busbee	Dem.	1975–1983
George W. Towns	Dem.	1847–1851	Joe Frank Harris	Dem.	1983–1991
Howell Cobb	Union (Dem.)	1851–1853	Zell Miller	Dem.	1991–1999
Herschel V. Johnson	Union (Dem.)	1853–1857	Roy Barnes	Dem.	1999–
Joseph E. Brown	Dem.	1857–1865			
James Johnson	Dem.	1865			

*Jeffersonian-Republican

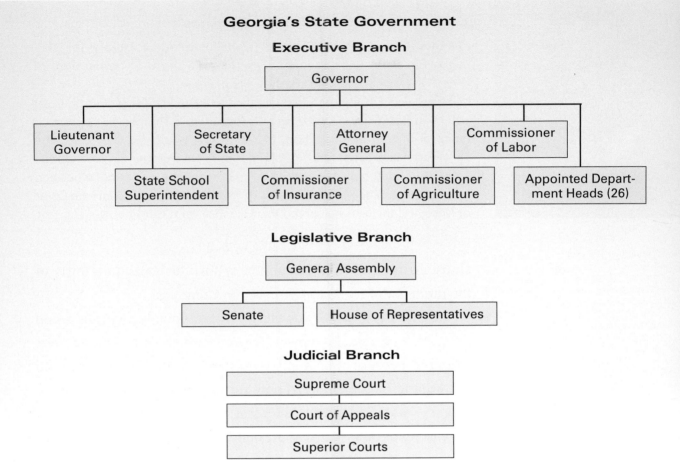

Georgia's State Government

Executive Branch

- Governor
  - Lieutenant Governor
  - Secretary of State
  - Attorney General
  - Commissioner of Labor
  - State School Superintendent
  - Commissioner of Insurance
  - Commissioner of Agriculture
  - Appointed Department Heads (26)

Legislative Branch

- General Assembly
  - Senate
  - House of Representatives

Judicial Branch

- Supreme Court
- Court of Appeals
- Superior Courts

Georgia in Washington

Two senators and eleven representatives are elected to represent Georgia in the U.S. Congress. Two Georgian representatives have been at the forefront in shaping America.

Carl Vinson (1883–1981) was born in Baldwin County and graduated from Mercer University Law School. Just fifteen days before his thirty-first birthday, he was sworn in as the youngest member of the U.S. House of Representatives. He was reelected for twenty-six consecutive terms. He also became chairman of the

Clarence Thomas

Clarence Thomas (1948–) was born in the Pin Point near Savannah. When he was seven years old, he went to live with his grandfather, who instilled in him the importance of having an education. In 1974, Thomas graduated from Yale Law School and became an assistant attorney general for the state of Missouri. In 1981, he served as the assistant secretary for civil rights in the U.S. Department of Education.

In 1990, President George Bush nominated Thomas as an associate justice of the U.S. Supreme Court. On October 23, 1991, Judge Thomas took his oath of office and became the fourth Supreme Court justice from Georgia. ■

House Armed Services Committee, a position he held for thirty of the more than fifty years he served in Congress.

"Uncle Carl," as he was known to everyone in Georgia, stood for a strong national defense. He even earned the nickname "The Admiral" because of his support for the navy. Vinson, however, did not want to be remembered only for his efforts to ensure that the country was always prepared for war. He said, "I devoutly hope that the casting of every gun and the building of every ship will be done with a prayer for the peace of America."

Congressman Newt Gingrich (1943–) was born in Pennsylva-

USS Carl Vinson

In 1973, President Richard Nixon announced that one of the country's first three nuclear-powered aircraft carriers would be named in honor of Congressman Carl Vinson. On March 15, 1980, Vinson became the first person in the history of the United States to watch a ship launched in his honor. In 1997, the 100,000-ton aircraft carrier traveled from California to her new home port in Puget Sound Naval Shipyard, Bremerton, Washington. There were 3,200 crew members aboard—including a cat named Heckel. ■

nia. Gingrich moved to Georgia and earned a bachelor of arts degree at Emory University. After obtaining master's and doctorate degrees at Tulane University, he returned to Georgia to teach history at West Georgia College.

Gingrich lost his first two attempts to be elected to Congress. In 1978, he was elected as a representative from Georgia's Sixth Congressional District. He became Speaker of the House of Representatives in 1995. He resigned this position in November 1998 after the Republican Party lost five seats in the House of Representatives during national elections.

Newt Gingrich was elected to Congress in 1978.

Presidential Perspectives

One U.S. president was born in Georgia, and one U.S. president died there. Both were Democrats, both served as state governors, and both are remembered as great humanitarian presidents.

Franklin Delano Roosevelt (1882–1945) first came to Warm Springs to vacation while he was the governor of New York. After he was elected the nation's thirty-second president in 1932, he often came to Warm Springs to relax from the stress of leading the country during the years of the Great Depression and World War II.

Roosevelt, who had been stricken with polio in 1921, enjoyed swimming in the soothing mineral waters of Warm Springs. He died on April 12, 1945, at his home in Warm Springs during his fourth term of office.

James Earl "Jimmy" Carter (1924–) was born in Plains. Carter graduated from the U.S. Naval Academy in 1946 and planned a career as a naval officer. In 1953, however, when his father died, Carter returned to Georgia to help with the family's peanut business.

Franklin Delano and Eleanor Roosevelt at their home in Warm Springs

Jimmy Carter, the thirty-ninth president of the United States

He entered politics and served in the Georgia Senate (1963–1967) and as the state's governor (1971–1975). In 1977, he took the oath of office as the thirty-ninth president of the United States.

Since leaving public office, former president Carter and his wife, Rosalynn, have dedicated their efforts to humanitarian causes. President Carter believes that these efforts have been some of the greatest accomplishments of his public-service career.

Making a Mark

Although there have been many landmark legal decisions in Georgia or involving Georgians, the case of *Chisholm* v. *Georgia* was one of the first and most important to have an impact on the nation.

In 1793, Alexander Chisholm, a South Carolina resident, filed suit against Georgia. He claimed that the state had confiscated his land during the Revolutionary War. Georgia argued against the right of the citizen to sue a state government and argued for the U.S. Supreme Court to take jurisdiction in the matter. The Supreme Court ruled in favor of Chisholm.

The suit resulted in the proposal of the Eleventh Amendment to the U.S. Constitution on March 4, 1794. The amendment prohibits

The Carter Center

The Carter Center in Atlanta is a nonprofit organization founded in 1982 by former president Jimmy Carter and Rosalynn Carter. The center is dedicated to resolving conflicts, promoting democracy, and fighting disease, hunger, oppression, and implementing solutions to global problems. The center is supported entirely by private funds. It is located 2 miles (3.2 km) east of downtown Atlanta, adjacent to the Jimmy Carter Library and Museum. ■

the use of federal courts for suits against a state by citizens of another state or of another nation. Although it was ratified in 1795, it was not proclaimed until 1798 because of delays in certifying the ratification.

Georgia's counties

The tiger swallowtail is Georgia's state butterfly.

The state flower, the Cherokee rose, honors the Cherokee Indians.

Georgia's State Symbols

State bird: Brown thrasher In 1935, Governor Eugene Talmadge proclaimed the brown thrasher Georgia's state bird. It was another thirty years before the Georgia Assembly made it official. The male brown thrasher has the largest repertoire of songs of any North American bird.

State butterfly: Tiger swallowtail The tiger swallowtail was adopted as the state butterfly in 1988. Some are on display at the Cecil B. Day Butterfly Center at Calloway Gardens near Pine Mountain, the largest glass-enclosed butterfly conservatory in the United States.

State flower: Cherokee rose In 1916, the National Society of the Daughters of the American Revolution nominated the Cherokee rose as Georgia's state flower to honor the Cherokee Indians who were forced to leave their lands in 1838. Horticulturists believe that this high-climbing shrub, which has waxy white petals around a large golden center, originated in China and was introduced to Georgia by the English in 1757. The Cherokee Indians widely distributed the hardy plant, which is used as a hedge throughout Georgia and other southern states.

State play: *Swamp Gravy* The folk play *Swamp Gravy* is a musical based on the tall tales and folklore of Miller County. It is named after a gravy, or soup, made from fried-fish drippings.

State vegetable: Vidalia onion The town of Vidalia sits in the center of a twenty-county region that has been designated—by state law and a federal marketing order—as the official Vidalia onion production area. Sulfur-deficient soils and mild temperatures give Vidalia onions their sweet taste.

State reptile: Gopher tortoise The gopher tortoise really digs Georgia. The tortoise makes long burrows for shelter in the sands of the coastal plain. Then, with true southern hospitality, the reptile shares the space with gopher frogs, indigo snakes, and toads.

State seashell: Knobbed whelk The knobbed whelk is a whorled shell with heavy spines, many knobs, and an orange or red opening. This shell is found all along Georgia's Atlantic shoreline. The minerals in the water create the colored markings on the sandy-colored, glossy surface of the shell.

State fruit: Peach Georgia is known for its state growers' reputation for producing the highest-quality fruit. The peach became the official state fruit in 1995.

State marine mammal: Right whale In 1985, this endangered species became Geor-gia's marine mammal. It is the only one of the great whales that is native to Georgia waters.

State wildflower: Azalea In 1979, the azalea was chosen as the state wildflower. The vibrant flowers of this hardy species bloom from March until August.

State mineral: Staurolite These crossed crystals, known as fairy crosses or fairy stones, are abundant in north Georgia. They have been collected as good-luck charms for generations.

State tree: Live oak The live oak was adopted in 1937. Some Georgians, however, believe the pine should be the state tree because there are more pine trees in Georgia than live oaks. The debate will probably never be resolved.

Georgia's state tree is the massive live oak.

Georgia's Nickname and Mottoes

The Georgia legislature has never designated an official state nickname, but Peach State and Empire State of the South are frequently used. Georgia has also been called the Goober State, referring to its role as a major peanut producer. An old nickname, Cracker State, was an unflattering term, possibly referring to poor, uneducated southern whites or to the days when whips with split tips were used to punish slaves.

Georgia has two state mottoes: "Wisdom, Justice, and Moderation," and "Agriculture and Commerce." Both are found on the state seal. ■

Georgia's State Seal

The Great Seal of Georgia was adopted in 1798. On one side of the seal are three pillars, which stand for the three branches of government. The pillars support an arch, which has the word "Constitution" inside it. A soldier with a drawn sword represents the military forces of the state. The words written on the ribbons wrapped around the pillars—"Wisdom," "Justice," and "Moderation"—are from the state pledge. In 1914, the date on the seal was changed from 1799 to 1776, the year of the Declaration of Independence.

On the reverse side of the seal is a view of a seashore, surrounded by the motto "Agriculture and Commerce." Within the scene is a ship at anchor bearing the U.S. flag. At a distance, a small boat travels from the interior of the state. The two ships represent the tobacco and cotton commerce of Georgia. A man plowing and a flock of sheep shaded by a tree represent the state's agriculture. ■

Georgia's State Flag

On October 16, 1879, the General Assembly passed a law requiring volunteer troops to carry "the flag of the State . . . as its battalion colors." The next day, Governor Alfred Colquitt approved Georgia's first official state flag. This flag contained a vertical blue band that covered one-third of the flag and three horizontal stripes—two scarlet and one white—across the other two-thirds. Small changes were made to the flag in 1902 and in 1914; the state seal was added sometime in the 1920s.

The present-day flag was adopted on July 1, 1956. The state seal is centered on a vertical blue band at one end of the flag; the battle flag of the Confederate States of America covers the rest of the banner. The official salute to the Georgia flag reads: "I pledge allegiance to the Georgia flag and to the principles for which it stands: Wisdom, Justice, and Moderation."

Some of Georgia's citizens are unhappy that the battle flag of the Confederate States of America is part of the state flag. In 1993, Governor Zell Miller tried to get the Georgia General Assembly to remove the battle flag, claiming that it did not represent the Georgia of today. Miller was not successful, however. The legislators felt that the battle flag appropriately honored those who fought and died for Georgia during the Civil War and should not be removed. ■

Georgia's State Song
"Georgia on My Mind"

In 1930, Stuart Gorrell penned the words and Hoagy Carmichael composed the music to "Georgia on My Mind." In 1960, Albany-born jazz and blues singer Ray Charles (below) made the song his first number-one hit, which earned him a Grammy Award. It was the first Grammy ever awarded to a Georgian by the National Academy of Recording Arts and Sciences. In 1979, "Georgia on My Mind" was adopted as the state song.

Melodies bring memories
That linger in my heart,
Make me think of Georgia
Why did we ever part?

Some sweet day, when blossoms fall
And all the world's a song,
I'll go back to Georgia
'Cause that's where I belong.

Georgia, Georgia, the whole day through,
Just an old sweet song keeps Georgia on
*   my mind.*
Georgia, Georgia, a song of you
Comes as sweet and clear as moonlight
*   through the pines.*

Other arms reach out to me,
Other eyes smile tenderly,
Still in peaceful dream I see
The road leads back to you.

Georgia, Georgia, no peace I find,
Just an old sweet song keeps Georgia on my mind. ■

CHAPTER EIGHT

Progress and Prosperity

What do peanut-butter cookies, T-shirts, fried chicken, pecan pie, peach cobbler, paper sacks, Coca-Cola, granite park benches, and jet airplanes have in common? They are all products of Georgia.

The Empire State of the South is more than just a popular nickname for Georgia. Empire comes from the Latin word meaning "to dominate." Since 1991, Georgia's economy has outperformed the nation's every year, sometimes by as much as 80 percent.

"Georgia, Where the World Does Business" is more than just a clever marketing slogan used by the state to invite new industry. Thirty-three foreign banks have offices in Georgia.

More than 2,000 new jobs are created each week in Georgia. During the 1990s, hundreds of international businesses, corporations, and organizations, including United Parcel Service, Holiday Inns, and the American Cancer Society, relocated their headquarters to Georgia.

Peanut farming is a $2 billion industry in Georgia.

Farming Is Big Business

In 1874, Georgia was the first state to establish a department of agriculture. Today, approximately 46,000 farms produce more than $6 billion in gross income and $1.3 billion in exports. In 1996, Georgia ranked twelfth among the states in cash receipts from sales of crops, livestock, poultry, and dairy products.

Opposite: As many as 22 million pounds (10 million kg) of apples are harvested in Georgia each year.

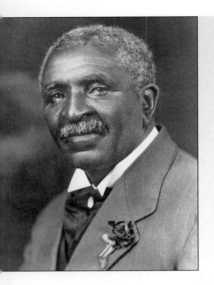

George Washington Carver

George Washington Carver (1864–1943) was born to slave parents in Diamond Grove, Missouri. In 1890, Carver entered Simpson College in Iowa, intending to study art. He transferred to Iowa State College of Agriculture (now Iowa State University) and earned a bachelor's degree and a master of science degree in agriculture.

As director of agricultural research at the Tuskegee Normal and Industrial Institute for Negroes (now Tuskegee University), Carver researched methods of crop rotation. One year, he planted peanuts; the next, he planted cotton. When his practices resulted in a surplus of peanuts, Carver developed 325 different uses for the peanut—including a type of printer's ink, soaps, dyes, and cosmetics. Carver is considered by many to be the father of the peanut industry. ■

Agricultural farmland covers 18,437 square miles (45,752 km) of Georgia, almost one-third of the state's total land area. There is more Georgia farmland than there is total land in Connecticut, Delaware, Massachusetts, and Rhode Island combined.

Not Just Peanuts

Peanuts are the largest cash crop in the state, the source of a $2 billion industry. About half of all the peanuts grown in the United States are grown by 8,000 farm families on 14,733 peanut farms in 69 counties. Another 37,000 Georgians work on peanut farms, in shelling plants, and in factories making peanut products.

In 1890, a doctor asked a storekeeper named George Bayle to grind some peanuts for people who could not chew. Bayle began selling his "nut butter" for six cents a pound. Peanut butter became popular when Joseph Rosefield patented a way to keep the oil from separating from the thick butter. Today, about 1 billion pounds (0.45 billion kg) of peanuts become peanut butter each year. One peanut-butter factory can produce 250,000 jars a day.

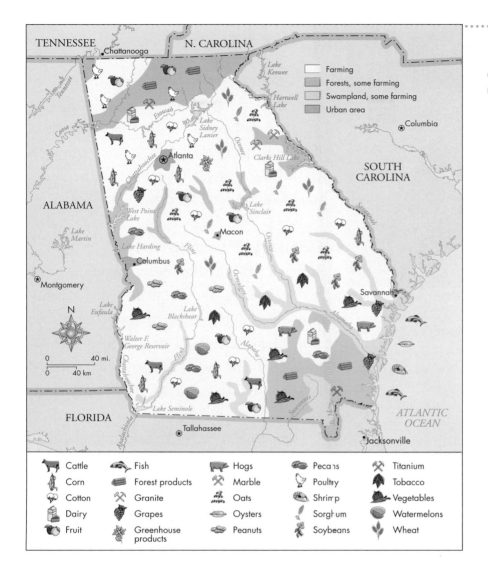

Map legend:

Georgia's natural resources
- Farming
- Forests, some farming
- Swampland, some farming
- Urban area

States and cities shown: TENNESSEE, Chattanooga, N. CAROLINA, Lake Keowee, Hartwell Lake, Columbia, SOUTH CAROLINA, Clarks Hill Lake, ALABAMA, Lake Martin, Lake Sidney Lanier, Atlanta, Lake Sinclair, Macon, West Point Lake, Lake Harding, Columbus, Montgomery, Lake Eufaula, Lake Blackshear, Walter F. George Reservoir, Savannah, Lake Seminole, FLORIDA, Tallahassee, Jacksonville, ATLANTIC OCEAN

Rivers: Tennessee, Coosa, Chattahoochee, Etowah, Oconee, Ocmulgee, Flint, Alapaha, Altamaha, Savannah, Suwannee, Apalachicola

Scale: 0 — 40 mi. / 0 — 40 km

N (compass rose)

Resource key:
- Cattle
- Corn
- Cotton
- Dairy
- Fruit
- Fish
- Forest products
- Granite
- Grapes
- Greenhouse products
- Hogs
- Marble
- Oats
- Oysters
- Peanuts
- Pecans
- Poultry
- Shrimp
- Sorghum
- Soybeans
- Titanium
- Tobacco
- Vegetables
- Watermelons
- Wheat

Cotton Counts

In 1997, Georgia produced more than 2 million bales of cotton—the largest harvest since 1918, valued at $728 million. Of Georgia's agriculture exports, cotton is second only to poultry and poultry products. Texas and California are the only states that produce more cotton than Georgia.

Canola Seed

The canola plant produces clusters of yellow, four-petaled flowers that develop green pods. The green pods, which contain tiny round seeds, ripen and turn brown. The seeds are then crushed to extract an edible oil valued for its nutritional qualities and especially for its low level of saturated fat. Canola oil is used in shortening, salad oils, and mayonnaise. Many movie theaters use canola-oil products when making popcorn.

Most of the canola grown in the United States is grown in the Midwest. In 1995, Georgia harvested its first crop of canola seed. ■

Cotton is also a food crop. Cottonseed oil, which has been produced in Georgia for the past 100 years, is used to make salad dressings, margarine, and various commercial oils for frying. Cotton hulls and seeds are used to make feed for cattle.

Poultry Production

Georgia ranks first in the nation in the number of chickens sold and in the value of broilers produced. In 1996, it produced more than 1 billion birds having a total value of $2.2 billion. The same year, Georgia raised 500,000 turkeys, which yielded 17 million pounds sold.

The state's egg production averages more than 4 billion eggs annually, which makes Georgia one of the nation's top ten egg producers. Sixty percent of Georgia's eggs are table eggs; 40 percent are hatching eggs.

Peaches and Pecans

Two counties in Georgia—Mitchell and Baconton—are credited with more pecan trees than any other place in the world. They produce an average of 1,000 pounds (454 kg) per acre, making Georgia the nation's leader in pecan production. Each year, about 90 million pounds (41 million kg) of pecans are grown in the state. If

you ate an entire pecan pie every day, it would take you more than 49,000 years to eat all the pecans grown in Georgia in one year.

About forty varieties of peaches grow on 12 million trees in the Peach State. In February and March of 1996, because of freezing temperatures and poor moisture, only 10 million pounds (4.5 million kg) of peaches were produced in Georgia. The year before, the state produced 160 million pounds (73 million kg).

Georgia's agricultural industry is one of the leading contributors to the state's $10 billion annual tourism industry. Visitors from all over the world tour apple orchards in Gilmer County, participate in Alma's Rabbit Eye Blueberry Festival, and enjoy slices of fruit at Cordele's Watermelon Festival. The Vidalia Onion Festival alone is estimated to generate millions of dollars annually.

What Georgia Grows, Manufactures, and Mines

Agriculture
Poultry
Cotton
Peanuts
Eggs
Hogs

Manufacturing
Textiles
Food products
Transportation equipment
Paper products

Mining
Clay
Crushed stone ■

Georgia Fruit Salad

Here is a sampling of the types and quantities of fruits produced in Georgia in one year. This information is from the U.S. Department of Agriculture's statistics for 1996.

Fruit	Acres (Ha) Planted	Pounds (Kg) Harvested
Blueberries	3,500 (1,418)	6 million (2.7 million)
Peaches	21,000 (8,505)	10 million (4.5 million)
Apples	2,400 (972)	22 million (10 million)
Watermelons	42,000 (17,010)	810 million (368 million)

Pine to Paper

In Georgia, money does grow on trees. In 1996, the state's sales of farm-forest products reached $150 million. Your paper lunch sack might once have been a piece of pine pulp in a Georgia forest. In addition to paper and timber products, the state's forests produce half of the world's supply of resins and turpentine.

Cola Clout

In 1886, business at Jacob's Pharmacy was booming. Sales of a new drink called Coca-Cola averaged thirteen a day. The inventor of the drink was James Pemberton (1831–1888), a pharmacist who had mixed the first recipe for the syrup in a pot behind his house in Marietta. Advertisements at the drugstore described the drink as "delicious and refreshing."

"Delicious and refreshing" also describes the impact that Pemberton's product has had on Georgia. In 1919, Ernest Woodruff paid $25 million to buy the rights to the Coca-Cola Company from Atlanta pharmacist Asa Candler. Woodruff's son, Robert, later sold stock. Today, the company earns $13 billion annually.

Woodruff reportedly locked the secret recipe away in an Atlanta bank vault. Fortunately, he did not lock away all the profits. Each year, donations from Woodruff's estate and from the Coca-Cola company provide millions of dollars for educational and cultural endeavors throughout Georgia.

A granite quarry near Elberton

Underground Treasures

The granite in one of Georgia's park benches is more than 300 million years old. It was mined in a quarry near Elberton in northeast Georgia. The granite deposit, which lies just below the earth's surface, is 6 miles (9.7 km) wide, 35 miles (56 km) long, and 3 miles (4.8 km) deep.

Granite is a tough rock composed of three different minerals: feldspar, quartz, and black mica. These minerals are easy to see because of their colors. The white mineral grains are feldspar. The light gray, glasslike grains are quartz. The black, flakelike grains are black mica.

There are forty-five granite quarries in Elberton, the Granite Capital of the World. In order to mine granite, a block is cut from the bed of the quarry with a jet piercing machine. The machine produces a jet of flame that burns at about 3,000°F (1,649°C), causing the granite to flake away in channels around the solid block.

The statue of Lincoln in the Lincoln Memorial is made of Georgia marble.

Explosives are used to mine larger blocks of granite—some 4 feet (1.2 m) high and deep, 8 feet (2.4 m) wide, and weighing as much as 10 tons. The large block is cut into smaller blocks with steel-cable-wire saws that have diamond segments. The blocks are lifted by crane to the finishing area, where they are smoothed and polished. About half of the large block will become material for tombstones, monuments, buildings, and benches. The other half will end up as street curbing, gravel, and grout.

Marble (crystalline calcium carbonate) is also mined in Georgia. The Georgia Marble Company, headquartered in Kennesaw in Long Swamp Valley, is the largest producer of marble in the world. Marble blocks mined from the largest open-pit quarry in the world weigh about 17 tons. The Long Swamp Valley quarries hold enough marble to last another 3,000 years.

Some of the nation's most famous landmarks, such as the statue of Lincoln in the Lincoln Memorial, are made of marble from Long Swamp Valley. The region's marble is also used in 300 different types of products, including the coating on chewing gum.

Ready for Takeoff

"Raptor one, ready for takeoff." That's how test pilot Paul Metz announced that he was about to hurtle the first F-22 Advanced Tactical Fighter (ATF) aircraft into the skies over Georgia. The F-22 Raptor, which takes its name from the word meaning "a bird of prey," can fly at more than twice the speed of sound. The F-22 ATF is the latest in a long line of American aircraft built by one of Georgia's largest industries, Lockheed Martin Aeronautical Systems in Marietta.

More than 9,000 people living in fifty-eight counties are employed by the aerospace company. Its annual payroll is more than $9 million. Lockheed Martin also employs 1,300 subcontractors within the state of Georgia.

Like the F-22 Raptor, Georgia is ready for takeoff. In everything from agriculture to aerospace industries, the state continues to grow as a powerful force in America's economy.

The F-22 Advanced Tactical Fighter, which is also called the Raptor

CHAPTER NINE

The Many Faces of Georgia

COLUMBUS
FIRE DEPT.
ENGINE

In 1790, when Thomas Jefferson delivered the first census of the United States to President George Washington, the census reported that 56,000 people lived in Georgia. Jefferson, however, estimated that the population was closer to 83,000.

Between 1870 and 1960, although more people left Georgia than moved in, the population increased because of a high birthrate. During the 1980s, the population increased by 19 percent.

By 1990, 200 years after the first census, Georgia had grown to 6,508,419 people. The 1990 census showed that, in addition to Atlanta, the cities of Columbus, Savannah, and Macon had populations greater than 100,000. By 1996, an estimated 7.4 million people lived in Georgia, making it the tenth-largest state in the United States in population.

Many people from other countries choose to live in Georgia. In 1996, more than 12,000 immigrants entering the United States stated that their intended place of residence was Georgia. Ethnically, the population is 71 percent white, 27 percent African-American, and 2 percent Hispanic, Asian, Native Americans, and others.

According to the 1990 census, Georgia had the tenth-largest population in the United States.

Coming and Going

The first immigrants to Georgia were from Asia. They crossed the Bering Strait more than 50,000 years ago. The Cherokee Indians, who spoke the Iroquoian language, probably migrated to Georgia

Opposite: A firefighter in Columbus

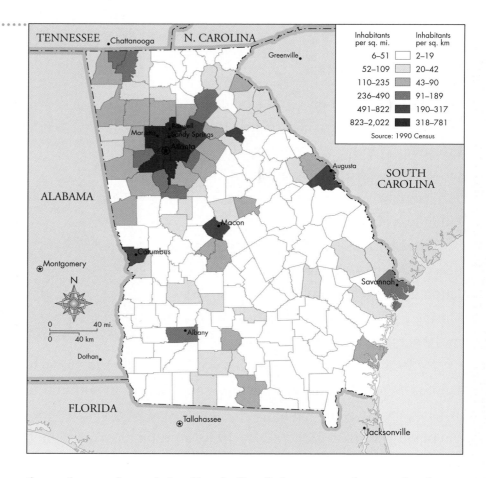

Georgia's population density

Inhabitants per sq. mi.		Inhabitants per sq. km
6–51		2–19
52–109		20–42
110–235		43–90
236–490		91–189
491–822		190–317
823–2,022		318–781

Source: 1990 Census

from the north, and the Creek Confederacy, made up of a dozen groups of Indians of Muskogean linguistic roots, migrated from what is now the southwestern United States. The Upper Creeks lived in central Georgia, the Lower Creeks lived in the south, and the Cherokee settled in the Appalachian Mountain region of northeast Georgia.

Bad Business

By the time the Europeans arrived in the mid-sixteenth century, about 10,000 people representing the five major southeastern Indian nations—Choctaw, Creek, Cherokee, Seminole, and Chickasaw—were living in Georgia. The Creek and Cherokee began trading with the colonists, who often took advantage of their lack of reading skills. The natives ended up in debt to the colony. To pay the debt, a group of Cherokees gave more than 2 million acres (0.8 million ha) of land to the colony.

Then, in 1828, gold was discovered near Dahlonega. As settlers rushed there to find their fortunes, the legal rights of the natives were ignored. The federal government forced 16,000 natives to leave their ancestral homes and move to Oklahoma. The Cherokee called this 116-day march *nunna-da-ul-tsun-yi,* meaning "the place where they cried." More than 4,000 people died of disease and starvation on the Trail of Tears during the winter of 1838–1839.

Striking gold in Georgia, 1828

Southern Sounds

English is the predominant spoken language in Georgia today. It is not unusual, however, to hear Spanish, Japanese, German, Norwegian, Chinese, French, and Taiwanese spoken in the larger metropolitan areas. The Georgia World Congress Center in Atlanta has facilities that provide simultaneous translation into six languages for international visitors who attend trade shows and meetings.

Gullah, a combination of West Indian, English, African, and Scots dialects, is still spoken on Sapelo Island. The island's residents are descendants of slaves brought from Africa to work on the sea islands' rice plantations before the Civil War. The Gullah, also

Deep Roots

The colony of Georgia was primarily settled by the English, Scottish, and Irish. Celebrating their Scottish and Irish heritage is still important to Georgia's residents. Savannah has the second-largest St. Patrick's Day parade and celebration in the nation. ■

R. J. Reynolds at his home on Sapelo Island in 1952

known as the Geechee people, remained on Sapelo Island after the Civil War to fulfill their dream of freedom.

Tobacco magnate R. J. Reynolds owned Sapelo Island from 1934 until his death in 1964. The island was then donated to the University of Georgia for the study of its wetland plants and animals. Today, Sapelo Island is the home of the National Estuarine Research Reserve—and still the home of the Gullah.

Southern Drawl

"Hi, y'all" is a phrase you will hear just about anywhere you go in Georgia. The phrase is part of what is known as the Southern drawl. Southern English is a style of English spoken at a slightly

Georgian Spoken Here

The language of Georgia's Native Americans lives in the names of the state's towns, rivers, and landmarks. Here are a few of the towns with Indian names and their tribal origins and meanings:

Apalachee Creek word meaning "those who lived beyond the mountain"

Cohutta Cherokee word meaning "frog"

Willacoochee Creek word meaning "little river"

Choestoe Cherokee word meaning "place where rabbits dance"

Although not Native American in origin, the following words and phrases are typical of the colorful expressions you'll hear throughout Georgia:

Gnat line An imaginary line running across the middle of Georgia. Anyone living "below the gnat line" lives in an area where the hot, moist summer weather that produces crops also produces plenty of insects.

Shoot the hooch Take a float trip on the Chattahoochee River

Catheads Biscuits

Fish house Casual eating place that serves seafood ■

slower speed than usual, with a soft, rounded emphasis on vowel sounds.

Regional dialects vary in Georgia from the "swamp sounds" of the Okefenokee, to the "mountain speak" of the Appalachians. Each dialect has its own unique vocabulary and spoken mannerisms, but all of them include the Southern drawl.

Education in Georgia

Groups of students in classrooms in Columbus, Augusta, and Tifton are listening carefully to the teacher—but the teacher is in a classroom in Statesboro. No, the teacher isn't shouting, and the students do not have exceptional hearing skills. They are all participating in a program known as "distance learning." Through satellite technology, students living almost anywhere in the state can expand their education beyond the limits of their local classrooms.

Education has come a long way since the days of Georgia's one-room rural schools, known as old field schools. Before 1872, most people in Georgia were educated in these types of schools. That year, however, Gustavos John Orr became the commissioner of education. Orr made sure that the public schools received the funds they had been promised by the state government. He is known as the father of the common-school system in Georgia.

Orr's commitment to public education continues in Georgia today. "My goal is to see that all children in Georgia's schools receive an education that allows them to develop their abilities to their fullest potential," said Linda C. Schrenko, state superintendent of schools, in 1997.

Georgia is committed to good education for its students.

During the 1990s, Georgia made great strides in spending for education.

Hope for Education

In 1992, Georgians voted for a constitutional amendment that designated that money from a state lottery be spent on education. As a result, in 1993, Georgia became the first state in the nation to provide free preschool for all four-year-old children. Each of the 1,800 elementary, middle, and high schools in Georgia now has its own satellite dish and related technology for distance-learning programs. Lottery receipts fund these programs.

Funds from the Georgia lottery have also paid for a program called HOPE (Helping Outstanding Pupils Educationally). Any Georgia student who maintains a B average in high school receives tuition assistance to attend any of the state's forty-eight senior colleges and universities, twenty-two community colleges, or thirty-two vocational-technical schools. In 1990, almost one-third of Georgia's residents age twenty-five and older did not have a high school diploma. By 1998, more than 300,000 Georgians were receiving higher education through HOPE.

Integration Efforts

In 1868, the state constitution was changed to provide public education for Georgia's African-American children for the first time. It took almost another 100 years for all the public schools in Georgia to open their doors to all children.

In 1960, a federal court order forced the integration of Atlanta's

The First Lotteries

In 1784 and 1785, the first lotteries were authorized in Georgia. They were held to raise money to build a hospital and a poorhouse for seamen in Savannah. Several more lotteries were authorized between 1790 and 1839 for a variety of public-works projects, including the construction of streets in Milledgeville, a courthouse in Screven County, and a fire department in Augusta. ■

public schools. In 1961, Charlayne Hunter and Hamilton Holmes were the first African-American students admitted to the University of Georgia. Hunter-Gault is now an award-winning television journalist, and Holmes was a noted surgeon before his death in 1995.

Hamilton Holmes and Charlayne Hunter, the first African-Americans to be admitted to the University of Georgia, on graduation day, 1963

Georgia in the News

In 1763, James Johnston, a Scots printer, established the *Georgia Gazette,* the first newspaper in Georgia. Johnston, who was the printer for the colony, continued to publish his paper for forty years. Most of the news was about events in England. Local news coverage included reprints of sermons and notices of deaths, piracies, and the arrivals of ships.

Sarah Hillhouse was the first woman in Georgia to edit and publish a newspaper. In 1803, when Sarah's husband died, she took over the printing of *The Monitor*. The newspaper, which had a circulation of about 800, focused on local and state events and

Miracle Lady

Martha McChesney Berry (1866–1942) began her career as an educator in a log cabin at Possom Trot, teaching children from poor families how to read. At that time, there were few public high schools in Georgia. In 1902, Berry started a private high school for boys on 83 acres (34 ha) of land she inherited. In 1909, she founded a similar school for girls.

In 1926, Martha turned her attention to establishing a junior college, and in 1930, added a four-year college. In 1972, Berry College established a graduate school.

Berry College has been called the Miracle on the Mountain. The college admits qualified students without regard to their ability to pay; the students work at the school to pay their tuition. Berry College in Mount Berry is rated as one of the top colleges in the world. ■

In 1785, Georgia became the first state to charter a state-supported university. The University of Georgia in Athens graduated its first class in 1804.

Highlights of Higher Education

Wesleyan College (left), founded in 1836 in Macon, was the first college in the world chartered to grant degrees to women.

Emory University, the largest private school in Georgia, is known as the university that Coca-Cola built. In 1979, Robert Woodruff, the owner of the Coca-Cola Company, gave Emory a $100 million endowment. Previously, he had given the university $110 million.

Morehouse College of Medicine, an all-male institution, grants degrees to physicians who will serve in the nation's rural and urban areas. In 1881, Spelman College, an all-female school, was the first college in the world to be chartered to grant degrees to black women. These colleges are two of the six schools that make up the Atlanta University Center, the largest African-American academic center in the nation. ■

people. Hillhouse also printed the official records of the state legislature.

From 1828 to 1834, the *Cherokee Phoenix* was printed in New Echota. It was printed in the Cherokee alphabet created by Sequoyah in 1821. This bilingual newspaper was the first paper in the United States published in a Native American language.

In 1868, the *Atlanta Constitution* was founded. By 1876, it had become one of the largest daily newspapers east of New Orleans, with a circulation of 140,000. It was called "the model newspaper of the southern states." Circulation increased significantly after 1893 when Georgia congressman Tom Watson obtained the first federal appropriations for Rural Free Delivery of mail.

Today, the *Atlanta Journal-Constitution,* with a daily circulation of 470,000, is the largest newspaper of Georgia's 29 daily and 143 weekly newspapers. Other large daily newspapers include the

Savannah Morning News, the *Columbus Ledger-Enquirer,* and the *Macon Telegraph.*

In 1922, WSB in Atlanta became Georgia's first radio station. Today, the state has more than 300 radio stations and 24 television stations.

Religion in Georgia

Native American sacred rituals were the first religious practices in Georgia. In 1566, Spanish missionaries introduced Catholicism, but the missionaries left after a century of effort. Today, less than 6 percent of those in Georgia who claim an affiliation with a church are Catholic.

The First Baptist Church in Dawsonville

European Protestants (such as Quakers and Puritans) and Jews all came to Georgia seeking religious freedom. When the colony was founded in 1733, Catholics and Jews were barred; however, these prohibitions were soon removed. In 1735, Jews in Savannah established the third-oldest Jewish congregation in North America.

In 1736, the first Protestant Sunday school in America was also founded in Savannah. That same year, German Lutherans founded the first orphanage in America. The Lutheran church built at New Ebenezer in 1736 is the oldest building in Georgia that is still intact and in use.

In 1788, the First Baptist Church in Savannah was established. It is believed to be the first African-American church in the United States. Baptists make up 60 percent of the state's church members. Methodists account for 15 percent. Other faiths make up the remaining 25 percent of Georgians with a religious affiliation.

CHAPTER TEN

The Arts, Architecture, and Athletics

t was 3 A.M., and Peggy Mitchell was wide awake. She knew it might seem rude to the girlfriend she was visiting to get up to write in the middle of the night, but Peggy didn't care. One of the stories that her grandfather had told her of his experiences during the Civil War burned inside her head. It was impossible to sleep. If she could just move some of those words out of her head and onto a piece of paper, she might finally be able to rest.

Years later, Peggy was still waking up with words burning inside her head. In 1925, she had given up her job as a newspaper

Margaret Mitchell, author of *Gone with the Wind*

reporter for the *Atlanta Journal* in order to recover from a severely sprained ankle. While recuperating, she secretly wrote page after page of a novel she was sure no one would ever want to read. She often spent all night at her typewriter in the kitchen of the tiny apartment—which she called "the Dump"—at 903 Crescent Avenue in Atlanta.

A friend finally convinced her to let an editor at Macmillan Publishing in New York read what she had spent seven years writing. The editor immediately bought the manuscript, which was published in 1936. The next year, *Gone with the Wind* earned its author, Margaret Munnerlyn "Peggy" Mitchell, an esteemed literary award—the Pulitzer Prize. Today, more copies of Mitchell's novel have been sold worldwide than of any other book except the Bible.

Opposite: A performance of *The Nutcracker* by the Atlanta Ballet

Flannery O'Connor, one of many acclaimed writers from Georgia

Georgia Writers

In 1835, Augustus Baldwin Longstreet became one of the most popular writers in the country when he published *Georgia Scenes*—sketches of his travels as a lawyer and judge throughout rural Georgia. Nineteenth-century poet Sidney Lanier tried to "paint a picture with words instead of brushes" in his poems about Georgia. Joel Chandler Harris relied on the stories of African folklore that he remembered from his childhood to write his first book, *Uncle Remus: His Songs and Sayings,* which was published in 1881. During the next fifteen years, Harris became famous for his books about Uncle Remus and the character Brer Rabbit.

Georgia-born writers Erskine Caldwell, Mary Flannery O'Connor, and Carson McCullers wrote many books and short stories about the South of the early twentieth century. Frank Yerby, an African-American writer born in Augusta, made his mark on the world of fiction in 1946, when he published his first book, *The Foxes of Harrow*. Since then, more than 50 million copies of Yerby's romance novels have been sold.

In 1966, Eliott Wigginton, a tenth-grade teacher at Rabun Gap High School, encouraged his students to gather stories about the folk arts, superstitions, and traditions of the local people. The first book in the collection, known as the *Foxfire* books, was published in 1972. It was a best-seller for thirty-five weeks. Many more in the series of *Foxfire* books have been published.

Georgia writers continue to produce best-selling books. Some of these well-known authors are Anne Rivers Siddons *(Peachtree Road),* Olive Ann Burns *(Cold Sassy Tree),* Terry Kay *(To Dance With the White Dog),* Eugenia Price *(Bright Captivity),* Bailey

The Pulitzer Prize

In 1864, Joseph Pulitzer (1847–1911) emigrated from Hungary to the United States. He served in a Union cavalry regiment until the end of the Civil War. Pulitzer then went to work as a reporter and, in 1883, purchased the *New York World* newspaper. The investment later made him very wealthy.

Through his will, Pulitzer left money to establish the Columbia University School of Journalism and the annual Pulitzer Prizes for literature, drama, music, and journalism. The Pulitzer Prize, considered the highest U.S. honor a writer can receive, has been awarded every year since 1917.

Pulitzer Prize recipients from Georgia are listed below:

Conrad Aiken (pen name: Samuel Jeake Jr.): *Selected Poems,* 1929
Caroline Walker: Novel, *Lamb in His Bosom,* 1934
Margaret Mitchell: Novel, *Gone with the Wind,* 1937
Ralph McGill: Newspaper Editorial, "A Church, a School," 1959
James Alan McPherson: Novel, *Elbow Room,* 1978
Alice Walker (right): Novel, *The Color Purple,* 1983
Alfred Uhry: Drama, *Driving Miss Daisy,* 1981
Mike Luckovich: Editorial cartoons, 1995 ■

White *(Mama Makes Up Her Mind),* Melissa Faye Green *(Praying for Sheetrock),* Pat Conroy *(Prince of Tides),* and John Berendt *(Midnight in the Garden of Good and Evil).*

Georgia on Film

Margaret Mitchell received $500,000 for the film rights to her novel *Gone with the Wind.* In 1939, when the movie opened in Atlanta, the average price for admissions to a movie theater in the United States was 25 cents. That night, a seat in the Loews Grand Theater cost $10. All of the theater's 2,031 seats were filled.

Since 1973, more than 300 movies have been filmed in Georgia. The state is a favorite location for filming authentic vintage homes, unique cemeteries, isolated beaches, and distinct mountain landscapes. The film industry has contributed more than $1.5 billion to Georgia.

Some of Georgia's most famous "movie stars" are cities like Covington and Commerce, two of the state's officially designated "Main Street cities," with downtown areas that have been restored to their original, historically accurate appearance. Savannah has been the site of many well-known movies, including *The Big Chill* (1982), *Glory* (1989), *Prince of Tides* (1990), *Forrest Gump* (1993), and *Midnight in the Garden of Good and Evil* (1997).

Music and Dance

Religious folk music in Bremen, opera in Atlanta, and country-and-western swing in Hiawassee, where the Georgia Music Fair is held each year—these are just some of the varied types of music sung, played, and listened to in Georgia. Songwriters and arrangers as diverse as Johnny Mercer and James Brown are honored at the Georgia Music Hall of Fame in Macon. Singers of sacred harp—a type of religious folk music that only uses voices—travel from all parts of Georgia to gather at outdoor camp meetings. Classical musicians come from as far away as Tokyo to play in Spivey Hall at Clayton State College in Morrow.

The roots of Georgia's music can be heard in McIntosh County, where the ring shout is still practiced. In 1993, the McIntosh County Singers were awarded a National Heritage Fellowship for continuing this African-American religious tradition of singing and clapping while moving in a circle.

Georgia's music roots are also found in Thomson at the Blind

Johnny Mercer is honored in the Georgia Music Hall of Fame.

Jessye Norman

Jessye Norman (1945–) was born in Augusta. By age six, she was singing and playing piano. She pursued her formal musical studies at Howard University in Washington, D.C., and Peabody Conservatory in Baltimore, Maryland. In 1969, she made her soprano operatic debut, then went on to win the hearts of audiences at Lincoln Center, Carnegie Hall, and in countries around the world.

The National Museum of Natural History in Paris named an orchid after Jessye Norman. The French awarded her the prestigious Legion of Honor. Norman is known not only for her opera skills but also for her vibrant renditions of gospel music. In 1997, the John F. Kennedy Center for Performing Arts awarded her a Kennedy Center Honor for her lifetime achievement in music. ■

Willie Blues Festival. The festival honors Willie McTell (1901–1959), who is considered the master of twelve-string guitar. Columbus-born Ma Rainey (1886–1939) is regarded as the Mother of the Blues. Chuck Leavell (1952–) is the acclaimed keyboardist for the rock group the Rolling Stones. He also owns Charlane Plantation, a tree farm near Macon, and has twice received the Georgia Tree Farmer Award of the Year from the Georgia Forestry Association. Rock groups the Indigo Girls, REM, and the B-52s, among others, also hail from Georgia.

Although the ring shout has almost become a lost art, the art of ballet is alive and well in Georgia. The Atlanta Ballet, founded in 1929, is the oldest ballet company in the United States and the largest independent arts organization in Georgia. The company offers free tickets to many of its performances to those who cannot afford to buy them. It also provides free dance lessons to elementary school children to improve the students' self-esteem and self-discipline.

Paintings and Pottery

During the Great Depression of the 1930s, a federal program called the Works Progress Administration (WPA) hired artists to paint murals in many Georgia communities. Water towers, bridges, post offices, and other WPA-funded construction projects provided "canvases" for some of Georgia's best-known artwork.

Mossy Creek potter Lanier Meaders makes face jugs—just one of the many types of pottery art that is crafted in Georgia. Families like the Hewells, Cravens, and Fergusons of Gillsville "hand-throw" (hand-shape) stoneware pottery. Each fall, thousands of visitors come to a "turning and burning" festival in Gillsville to watch three generations of these families, all working from the same batch of Georgia clay, create pottery pieces that will represent Georgia all over the world.

Skilled artists from Georgia's Appalachian regions produce baskets, woodcarvings, paintings, and pottery that represent their unique mountain cultures. African-American art is displayed throughout Georgia in galleries and museums, such as Savannah's Beach Institute, which was organized in 1865 to educate freed slaves.

Artful Architecture

Architecture as art is a long and continuing tradition in Georgia. In the wards, streets, and lanes of many of Georgia's cities, there are examples of Colonial, Federal, Greek Revival, Italianate, and Victorian period buildings. Some of the earliest buildings were constructed from "tabby"—a mixture of crushed oyster shells, lime, and sand—but bricks of red Georgia clay and wood from Georgia's forests were most frequently used.

Sermon Art

Howard Finster (1916–) retired as a preacher in 1965. He began making what he calls his "sermon art" in 1976. Finster uses all sorts of junk to make the sculptures and paintings that he displays at Paradise Gardens near Summerville. Paradise Gardens is one of Georgia's top ten tourist attractions. There are more than 42,000 pieces of Finster folk art on display at Paradise Gardens. Collectors prize their "Finster finds." Some of his works are also part of the collection of the Smithsonian Institution's National Museum of American Art. ■

The Robert W. Woodruff Arts Center in Atlanta is home to the Atlanta Symphony Orchestra, the Alliance Theatre Company, and the High Museum of Art. Performance art and visual art come together within this impressive modern facility, which is itself a work of art. The American Institute of Architects called the Woodruff Arts Center one of the ten best works of American architecture.

An 1819 mansion houses the Telfair Academy of Arts and Sciences in Savannah. The Telfair mansion was bequeathed to the Georgia Historical Society by Mary Telfair, the daughter of Georgia governor Edward Telfair. The building is an excellent example of architecture from the English Regency period (1800–1820).

The Telfair Academy of Arts and Sciences in Savannah is just one example of Georgia's exquisite architecture.

121

Athletics Abound

According to legend, the Native American people in northwest Georgia used sticks and balls to settle boundary disputes along the Etowah River, playing a game the Cherokees called "little brother to war." In 1892, "football fever" hit Georgia when the University of Georgia beat Mercer College with the score 50–0. In 1901, the first minor league baseball team was formed in Georgia. In 1975, the Macon Whoopees began playing minor league professional ice hockey.

Sticks, balls, and football fever are still a big part of life in Georgia—but so are many other games. Harness racing, hot-air ballooning, and hunting-dog competitions are the favorite activities of thousands of Georgians. Motor sports, boating, and fishing are also at the top of the list.

Habitat for Humanity International

Habitat for Humanity International is headquartered in Americus. This nonprofit housing ministry was founded in 1976 by Millard and Linda Fuller. Its purpose is to provide adequate, comfortable shelter to the homeless. The organization relies on volunteer labor and private donations.

Habitat for Humanity International has 1,300 chapters in the United States and fifty-six other countries. More than 20,000 houses have been built or renovated, and 800 construction projects are underway at any time. The organization's best-known construction volunteer is former president Jimmy Carter. ■

Ted Turner

Robert Edward "Ted" Turner (1938–) was born in Cincinnati, Ohio. He attended Brown University in Providence, Rhode Island, where he was president of the Yacht Club and the Debate Club. In 1963, he moved to Georgia to manage his father's billboard business.

In 1970, Turner purchased a small, independent television station in Atlanta. In 1980, he launched the twenty-four-hour Cable News Network (CNN) from Atlanta. CNN, the first global television news company, is broadcast in more than 200 countries. Turner's broadcast holdings have since expanded to include numerous entertainment and sports networks.

Turner is an avid sportsman and sports fan. In 1977, he won the America's Cup yacht race. He started the Goodwill Games competition between the United States and Russia. His company, Turner Broadcasting Systems, Inc., owns the Atlanta Braves, Atlanta Hawks, and Atlanta Thrashers sports teams. ■

Professional Sports

Georgia is the home of football's Atlanta Falcons, baseball's Atlanta Braves, and basketball's Atlanta Hawks. The Atlanta Thrashers is the state's newest professional sports franchise, a National Hockey League team that began playing in 1999.

The Atlanta Hawks make their home in the $213 million Atlanta Arena. The Falcons play football in the Georgia Dome, and the Braves are at home in the new Turner Field.

Super Sports

In 1994, Georgia hosted Super Bowl XXVIII at the Georgia Dome in Atlanta. That one event created hundreds of new jobs and generated $166 million for Georgia. Super Bowl XXXIV, which will take place in 2000, will also be played in Atlanta.

Women Win the Gold

A heat wave enveloped Golden Park Stadium in Columbus as the U.S. women's softball team took the field in 1996. The team's coach was seventy-two-year-old Ralph Raymond. In the ninth inning, pitcher Lisa Fernandez struck out Xu Jian of China. The United States had a 3–1 win—and the first Olympic gold medal ever awarded for softball. ■

The Olympic Stadium in downtown Atlanta

Since 1934, Georgia has been the home of the Masters Tournament, which is held each year at Augusta National Golf Club. The golf course was built by world-famous Georgia golfer Robert Tyre "Bobby" Jones Jr. (1902–1971). In 1930, at age twenty-eight, Jones made history as the first and only golfer ever to win all four of the top golf tournaments in the world in a single year—known as the Grand Slam of golf.

Olympic Outcomes

"If you saw the Olympics, you saw Georgia." That was what one reporter wrote after covering some of the the 271 events of the 1996 Summer Olympic Centennial Games. Most of the competitions were held at the new Olympic Stadium built in downtown Atlanta. Many events, like rowing, volleyball, and soccer, were held in other locations throughout the state.

There were 1,933 medals awarded to the world's top athletes who competed in the 1996 Summer Olympic Centennial Games. The best prize, however, went to Georgia: The new Centennial Stadium became Turner Field, home of the Atlanta Braves baseball team.

Turner Field features an entertainment area, where visitors can practice their pitching and batting skills; a Braves Museum and

Sports Greats

Tyrus Raymond "Ty" Cobb [right] (1886–1961) was born near Narrows. Known as the Georgia Peach, he was one of the first five men elected to the National Baseball Hall of Fame.

Jack Roosevelt "Jackie" Robinson (1919–1972) was born in Cairo. On April 15, 1947, as first-base man for the Brooklyn Dodgers, he became the first African-American to play in the major leagues.

Melvin Carnell "Mel" Blount (1948–) was born in Vidalia. He helped the Pittsburg Steelers win four Super Bowls and was inducted into the Pro Football Hall of Fame in 1989.

Walt Frazier (1945–) was born in Atlanta. He led the New York Knicks basketball team to two National Basketball Association (NBA) championships. He was a seven-time NBA All-Star before he was inducted into the Basketball Hall of Fame. ■

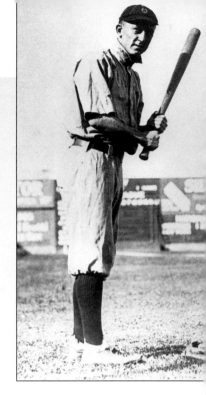

Hall of Fame; and Tooner Field, where cartoon characters Homer and Rally greet young Braves fans. The stadium has 130,000 square feet (52,650 ha) of playing turf and 49,714 seats for spectators.

Moving On

In 1996, Mary Hood, of the Georgia Humanities Council Writing Project, wrote: "For a moment we have felt it—the kinship with the ones who stood here before us, and the ones who will come after. Sooner or later, we do move on, in space or in time. Someone will come after us because that is what makes the future."

The Georgia of today will someday be the Georgia of the past, making way for the Georgia of the future. That continuity of people, accomplishments, and events is what keeps Georgia on the move.

Timeline

United States History

The first permanent British settlement is established in North America at Jamestown.	**1607**
Pilgrims found Plymouth Colony, the second permanent British settlement.	**1620**
America declares its independence from England.	**1776**
Treaty of Paris officially ends the Revolutionary War in America.	**1783**
U.S. Constitution is written.	**1787**

Georgia State History

1540 Spanish explorer Hernando de Soto travels through the lands that are now Georgia in search of gold.

1566 Pedro Menéndez de Avilés establishes a mission and fort on Saint Catherines Island.

1686 The Spanish abandon the Georgia coast to English colonists from Carolina.

1732 James Edward Oglethorpe and twenty other men secure a royal charter for the colony of Georgia from King George II.

1733 Savannah becomes the first European settlement in Georgia.

1742 The English victory in the Battle of Bloody Marsh removes the Spanish from Georgia.

1763 Spain cedes Florida to England and establishes Georgia's boundary at St. Marys River. Georgia's boundaries with the Creek Nation are established.

1777 Georgia's first constitution is adopted.

1787 Border with South Carolina is established.

1788 On January 2, Georgia becomes the fourth state to ratify the Constitution of the United States of America.

1793 Eli Whitney invents the cotton gin.

United States History

Louisiana Purchase almost doubles **1803**
the size of the United States.

U.S. and Britain **1812–15**
fight the War of 1812.

The North and South fight **1861–65**
each other in the American Civil War.

The United States is **1917–18**
involved in World War I.

Stock market crashes, plunging the **1929**
United States into the
Great Depression.

The United States fights in **1941–45**
World War II.

The United States becomes a **1945**
charter member of the
United Nations.

The United States fights **1951–53**
in the Korean War.

The U.S. Congress enacts a series of **1964**
groundbreaking civil rights laws.

The United States **1964–73**
engages in the Vietnam War.

The United States and other **1991**
nations fight the brief Persian
Gulf War against Iraq.

Georgia State History

1802 Georgia cedes to the United States all
the land west of the Chattahoochee
River and Nickajack Creek and north of
the 31st parallel.

1861 On January 19, Georgia secedes from
the Union and joins the Confederacy.

1866 Border with Florida is established.

1868 Atlanta becomes the state capital.

1870 On July 15, Georgia is readmitted to
the Union.

1883 Boundary with Alabama is established.

1920 Women in Georgia vote for the first
time.

1924 The boll weevil, which had been
destroying crops since before World
War II, is finally destroyed by crop
dusters.

1943 Georgia becomes the first state to
allow eighteen-year-olds to vote.

1960 A federal court order forces the integration of Atlanta's public schools.

1976 Former Georgia governor Jimmy
Carter is elected the thirty-ninth president of the United States.

1981 A new state constitution is adopted.

1996 The Summer Olympic Centennial
Games are held in Atlanta.

Fast Facts

Atlanta

Statehood date	January 2, 1788, the 4th state
Origin of state name	Named for King George II of England by James Oglethorpe, colonial administrator
State capital	Atlanta
State nicknames	Peach State, Empire State of the South
State motto	"Wisdom, Justice, and Moderation"
State bird	Brown thrasher
State flower	Cherokee rose
State insect	Honeybee
State butterfly	Tiger swallowtail
State marine mammal	Right whale
State crop	Peanut
State reptile	Gopher tortoise
State fish	Largemouth bass
State seashell	Knobbed whelk
State fossil	Shark tooth
State fruit	Peach

Live oak

Savannah River

State game bird	Bobwhite quail
State wildflower	Azalea
State gem	Quartz
State mineral	Staurolite
State song	"Georgia on My Mind"
State tree	Live oak
State fair	Perry (October)
Total area; rank	58,977 sq. mi. (152,750 sq km), 24th
Land; rank	57,919 sq. mi. (150,010 sq km), 21th
Water; rank	1,058 sq. mi. (2,740 sq km), 28th
Inland water; rank	1,011 sq. mi. (2,618 sq km), 20th
Coastal water; rank	47 sq. mi. (122 sq km), 18th
Geographic center	Twiggs, 18 miles (29 km) southeast of Macon
Latitude and longitude	Georgia is located approximately between 35° 00' and 30° 42' N and 80° 53' and 85° 36' W
Highest point	Brasstown Bald Mountain, 4,784 feet (1,458 m)
Lowest point	Sea level at the Atlantic Ocean
Largest city	Atlanta
Number of counties	159
Longest river	Savannah River, 350 miles (563 km)
Population (rank)	6,508,419 (1990 census); 11th
Density	110 persons per sq. mi. (43 per sq km)

Schoolchildren

Population distribution	63% urban, 37% rural	
Ethnic distribution	White	71.01%
(does not equal 100%)	African-American	26.96%
	Hispanic	1.68%
	Asian and Pacific Islanders	1.17%
	Native American	0.21%
	Other	0.65%

Record high temperature	113°F (45°C) at Greenville on May 27, 1978
Record low temperature	–17°F (–27°C) at Floyd County on January 27, 1940
Average July temperature	80°F (27°C)
Average January temperature	47°F (8°C)
Average yearly precipitation	50 inches (127 cm)

Natural Areas and Historic Sites

National Military Park

Chickamauga-Chattanooga National Military Park memorializes Civil War battle sites.

National Battlefield Park

Kennesaw Mountain National Battlefield Park is the site of a number of Civil War battles during the Atlanta campaign.

Coastal sea oats

National Monuments

Fort Frederica National Monument was built during the conflict between Britain and Spain over the control of southeastern territories.

Fort Pulaski National Monument is a masonry fort bombarded by the Union army during the Civil War.

Ocmulgee National Monument preserves artifacts of ancient cultures from Ice Age peoples to the Creek.

National Historic Sites

Martin Luther King Jr. National Historic Site is the birthplace and grave site of the civil rights leader.

Jimmy Carter National Historic Site is the family home of the thirty-ninth president of the United States.

National Seashore

Cumberland Island National Seashore is the largest of Georgia's Golden Isles seashores.

National Scenic Trail

The Appalachian Trail is a 2,158-mile (3,473-km) trail extending the length of the Appalachian Mountains from Maine to Georgia.

National Forests

Chattahoochee National Forest is a scenic area of mountains (including Brasstown Bald Mountain, the highest spot in the state), lakes, and forests in northern Georgia.

Oconee National Forest is in central Georgia.

State Parks

Georgia has fifty-nine state parks and historic sites.

The Chattahoochee National Forest

Sports Teams

NCAA Teams (Division I)

Georgia Southern University Eagles

Georgia State University Panthers

Georgia Tech Yellow Jackets

Mercer University Bears

University of Georgia Bulldogs

Major League Baseball

Atlanta Braves

National Basketball Association

Atlanta Hawks

National Football League

Atlanta Falcons

National Hockey League

Atlanta Thrashers

Cultural Institutions

Libraries

Georgia State Library and State Archives (Atlanta)

DeRenne Library at the University of Georgia (Athens)

Georgia Historical Society Library (Savannah)

Museums

High Museum of Art (Atlanta) has an important collection of European masters and early and contemporary American art.

Georgia Museum of Art at the University of Georgia (Athens) has a fine collection of American art.

Atlanta Ballet

The Atlanta History Center is one of the nation's largest urban museums and has exhibits on the Civil War and the history of Atlanta.

Performing Arts

Georgia has two major opera companies, two major symphony orchestras, one major dance company, and one major professional theater company.

Universities and Colleges

In the mid-1990s, Georgia had seventy-two public and forty-four private institutions of higher learning.

Annual Events

January–March

Fasching Karnival in Helen (mid-January)

Georgia Day in Savannah (February 12)

Rattlesnake Roundup in Claxton (early March)

Cherry Blossom Festival in Macon (mid-March)

Statewide Tours of Homes and Gardens (late March and early April)

April–June

Masters Tournament at Augusta National Golf Course (April)

Riverfest Weekend in Columbus (April)

Dogwood Festival in Atlanta (early April)

Thomasville Rose Festival (late April)

Georgia Renaissance Festival in Fairburn and Peachtree City (late April)

Stay and See Georgia, Stone Mountain Park, Atlanta (early May)

Andersonville Historic Fair (May)

Blessing of the Shrimp Fleet in Brunswick (May)

Vidalia Onion Festival (mid-May)

Macon cherry blossoms

July–September

Georgia Shakespeare Festival in Atlanta (early July)

Homespun Festival in Polk County (July)

Georgia Mountain Fair in Hiawassee (August)

Beach Music Festival on Jekyll Island (mid-August)

Powers Crossroads Arts and Crafts Festival in Newnan (Labor Day weekend)

Arts Festival of Atlanta (mid-September)

Barnesville Buggy Days (September)

October–December

Andersonville Historic Fair in Andersonville (October)

Georgia National Fair in Perry (October)

Gold Rush Days in Dahlonega (October)

Oktoberfest Celebration in Helen (October)

Prater's Mill Country Fair near Dalton (October and May)

Christmas on Jekyll Island (December)

Marietta Pilgrimage in Marietta (December)

Jekyll Island

Famous People

Conrad Aiken (1889–1973)	Poet and author
Julian Bond (1940–)	Politician and civil rights leader
James Nathaniel (Jim) Brown (1936–)	Football player
Erskine Preston Caldwell (1903–1987)	Author
Asa Griggs Candler (1851–1929)	Pharmacist, businessman, and philanthropist

Martin Luther King Jr.

Ted Turner

James Earl (Jimmy) Carter (1924–)	U.S. president
Tyrus Raymond (Ty) Cobb (1886–1961)	Baseball player
John Charles Frémont (1813–1890)	Soldier
Joel Chandler Harris (1848–1908)	Author and journalist
Maynard Holbrook Jackson (1938–)	Politician
Martin Luther King Jr. (1929–1968)	Religious leader and social reformer
Sidney Lanier (1842–1881)	Poet and critic
Crawford Williamson Long (1815–1878)	Surgeon
Juliette Gordon Low (1860–1927)	Founder of the Girl Scouts of America
Carson McCullers (1917–1967)	Author
Margaret Mitchell (1900–1949)	Author
Flannery O'Connor (1925–1964)	Author
Jack Roosevelt (Jackie) Robinson (1919–1972)	Baseball player
John Ross (1790–1866)	Cherokee chief
Sequoyah (1760–1843)	Silversmith and inventor of Cherokee alphabet
Robert Edward (Ted) Turner III (1938–)	Broadcasting and sports executive
Andrew Jackson Young Jr. (1932–)	Civil rights leader and politician

To Find Out More

History

- Fradin, Dennis Brindell. *Georgia*. Chicago: Childrens Press, 1991.

- Fradin, Dennis Brindell. *The Georgia Colony*. Chicago: Childrens Press, 1989.

- Knorr, Rosanne. *Kidding Around Atlanta: A Fun Filled, Fact Packed Travel & Activity Book*. Santa Fe: John Muir, 1997.

- Ladoux, Rita C. *Georgia*. Minneapolis: Lerner, 1991.

- Lerner Geography Staff. *Georgia*. Minneapolis: Lerner, 1993.

- Wills, Charles A. *A Historical Album of Georgia*. Brookfield, Conn.: Millbrook, 1996.

Fiction

- Beatty, Patricia. *Turn Homeward, Hannalee*. New York: William Morrow & Company, 1984.

- Gibbons, Faye, and Faye Ronald Himler (illustrator). *Hook Moon Night: Spooky Tales from the Georgia Mountains*. New York: William Morrow & Company, 1997.

Biographies

- Bergman, Irwin. *Jackie Robinson*. Broomall, Penn.: Chelsea House, 1994.

- Haskins, Jim. *I Have a Dream: The Life and Words of Martin Luther King*. Brookfield, Conn.: Millbrook Press, 1992.

- Lazo, Caroline. *Jimmy Carter: On the Road to Peace*. Englewood Cliffs, N.J.: Silver Burdett, 1996.

- Lyons, Mary E. *Stitching Stars: The Story Quilts of Harriet Powers*. New York: Atheneum, 1993.

- Ward, Linda R. *Jimmy Carter: Thirty-ninth President of the United States*. Chicago: Childrens Press, 1989.

Websites

- **Georgia Capitol Museum**
  http://www.sos.state.ga.us/ museum/html/georgia_ capitol_museum.html
  Complete information on Georgia's natural resources, state symbols, history, people, and flags

- **Georgia State Website**
  http://www.state.ga.us/
  Information on state government, travel, tourism, education, and much more

- **Georgia History Page**
  http://www.cviog.uga.edu/ projects/gainfo/gahist.htm
  Information on Georgia's history, from the prehistoric period through the twentieth century, including diaries and historical documents and information on the railroads

Addresses

- **Georgia Department of Industry, Trade and Tourism**
  PO Box 1776
  Atlanta, GA 30301
  For trade and tourism information about Georgia

- **Office of the Secretary of State**
  214 State Capitol
  Atlanta, GA 30334
  For information on the government and history of Georgia

Index

Page numbers in *italics* indicate illustrations.

Photo Credits

Photographs ©:

AP/Wide World Photos: 28, 45, 87 bottom, 108, 111, 116, 125, 132
Archive Photos: 36 (American Stock), 48, 135 top (CNP), 13, 35, 115
Aristock, Inc.: 121 top (John & Betsy Braden), 7 top center, 17 top, 77 (Robb Helfrick), 7 bottom center, 91 bottom (Dorothy Hibbert Krakow), 95 (Gordon Kilgore), 88, 110 (Michael A. Schwarz), 113 (John Slemp), 58 bottom, 131 top (Carl Alan Smith)
Bob Clemenz Photography: 39 right (Bob & Suzanne Clemenz)
Corbis-Bettmann: 86 top, 122 (Reuters), 86 bottom, 118 (UPI), 9 (Ward/Baldwin), 10
David R. Frazier: 7 top right, 7 top left, 41, 58 top, 67, 68, 71, 79, 101, 104
Delta Air Transit Heritage Museum, Inc.: 43
Dembinsky Photo Assoc.: 90 top (Stan Osolinski)
Envision: 73 (David Bishop)
Gamma-Liaison: 117 (Evan Agostini), 93 (Alain Benainous), 119 (Robert Giroux), 87 top (Erik Lesser)
Georgia Historical Society: 17 bottom (Cordray-Foltz Collection), 30, 37, 47
H. Armstrong Roberts, Inc.: 94 (H. Abernathy), 6 center top, 98 (Blumebild)
James P. Rowan: 15, 62
Lockheed Martin: 103
New England Stock Photo: 57, 90 bottom (Carol Christensen), 66, 128 (Jean Higgins)
North Wind Picture Archives: 6 bottom, 8, 12, 21, 22, 24, 27, 29, 34, 40, 76, 107, 129 bottom
PhotoEdit: 70 (Bachmann)
Reproduced with Permission from the Office of the Governor, State of Georgia: 92
Ron Sherman: 6 top left, 44, 49, 51, 53, 65, 81, 83, 109, 114, 123, 124, 130, 133 top, 135 bottom
Stock Montage, Inc.: 14, 19, 32, 33, 96
Stone Mountain Memorial Association: 39 left
Superstock, Inc.: 7 bottom, 105, 121 bottom
Terry Donnelly: 2, 50, 91 top, 129 top, 134
The Davey Tree Expert Co.: 56 (Albin P. Dearing, V.)
The Museum of Arts and Sciences, Macon, GA: 52
Tom Dietrich: 102
Tom Till: 54
Tony Stone Images: cover (Ken Biggs), 80 (John Elk), 82 (Chuck Pefley), back cover, 63 (James Randklev)
Unicorn Stock Photos: 99 (Jean Higgins), 59, 131 bottom (Andre Jenny), 6 top right, 26 (H. Schmeiser)
Viesti Collection, Inc.: 60 (Tara Darling), 74, 133 bottom (M. C. Price)
Wesleyan College: 112 (Michael A. Schwarz)
Wildwater Ltd. Rafting: 75.
Maps by XNR Productions, Inc.

6258-8630